MW00856913

De
to
a Dif
Dire

We've Decided to Go in a Different Direction

Essays

Tess Sanchez

Gallery Books

New York   Amsterdam/Antwerp   London
Toronto   Sydney/Melbourne   New Delhi

G

Gallery Books
An Imprint of Simon & Schuster, LLC
1230 Avenue of the Americas
New York, NY 10020

For more than 100 years, Simon & Schuster has championed authors and the stories they create. By respecting the copyright of an author's intellectual property, you enable Simon & Schuster and the author to continue publishing exceptional books for years to come. We thank you for supporting the author's copyright by purchasing an authorized edition of this book.

No amount of this book may be reproduced or stored in any format, nor may it be uploaded to any website, database, language-learning model, or other repository, retrieval, or artificial intelligence system without express permission. All rights reserved. Inquiries may be directed to Simon & Schuster, 1230 Avenue of the Americas, New York, NY 10020 or permissions@simonandschuster.com.

Copyright © 2025 by Tess Sanchez

All rights reserved, including the right to reproduce this book or portions thereof in any form whatsoever. For information, address Gallery Books Subsidiary Rights Department, 1230 Avenue of the Americas, New York, NY 10020.

First Gallery Books hardcover edition April 2025

GALLERY BOOKS and colophon are registered trademarks of Simon & Schuster, LLC

Simon & Schuster strongly believes in freedom of expression and stands againstcensorship in all its forms. For more information, visit BooksBelong.com.

For information about special discounts for bulk purchases, please contact Simon & Schuster Special Sales at 1-866-506-1949 or business@simonandschuster.com.

The Simon & Schuster Speakers Bureau can bring authors to your live event. For more information or to book an event, contact the Simon & Schuster Speakers Bureau at 1-866-248-3049 or visit our website at www.simonspeakers.com.

Interior design by Hope Herr-Cardillo

Manufactured in the United States of America

10   9   8   7   6   5   4   3   2   1

Library of Congress Cataloging-in-Publication Data is available.

ISBN 978-1-6680-6085-8
ISBN 978-1-6680-6087-2 (ebook)

*To Max, meeting you is the single best thing
that has happened in my life from which
all beautiful things have grown.*

Contents

Foreword by Max Greenfield   ix

1. Casting the Intern: Co-Star Billing   1
2. Red Wool Beanie: Shared Card   25
3. Casting: The Big Leagues   43
4. Broken Picker: And Why I DM'd Britney Spears   61
5. Pablo: Star of the Feature   77
6. Tío: One of One   89
7. Click to Join This Zoom: Series Cancellation   101
8. Striking the Set: Painful Favor   111
9. Head of Operations: The H Suite   125
10. Shoeless: Barefoot Babes in Turnaround   143
11. Cycle of Life: Syndication   155
12. The Plus-One Era: N/I (as in, Not Interested)   173
13. Callbacks for Sexy Mamis: Recurring Guest Star   185
14. Exit Strategy: Releasing the Breakdown   199
15. End Credits   215

Epilogue: State of Affairs: STARS, Where Are They Now?   225

Spotify Playlist   231

Acknowledgments   233

Author's Note   237

Foreword

Hello, reader. My name is Mr. Tess Sanchez. And I write that with pride and some degree of legality.

I offered to write this foreword because Tess was venting a lot about this particular assignment from her editor. While she loves introductions in life, she's not a fan of them in books. She just wants to jump in and get to the heart of the matter (something about a preview taking up too much real estate). As Tess continued her rant about this for several days, I finally had heard enough, insisting, "Please, allow me to do this for you." This is kind of how our relationship works. Tess won't ask for help but will loudly debate something, sometimes up to a week or more, and as a result, I write a foreword. Truthfully, I am honored to be doing so.

Who better to introduce you to Tess than me, the person who has been by her side for more than twenty years. She is the stylish and witty author of the book you are about to read. She is also the incredible mother of our two kids, and best of all, a really good time. An arrive-early, stay-late kind of person. She is refreshingly authentic and unafraid to ask the revealing questions that other people shy away from, because she is genuinely interested in other people. She has the confidence and optimism of Reese's Elle Woods meets the funky realness of J. Lo's Jenny from the Block, meets the busybody-ness of Mindy Kaling's Kelly Kapoor.

Tess is also equal parts warm sounding board and nosy meddler. She is disarming and affable, so much so, that people find themselves sharing their most intimate secrets with her. Her dentist recently came out to her during a routine cleaning. But for Tess, that is just a regular Tuesday. When it comes to meddling, she thinks nothing of returning an email on my behalf, or on behalf of our daughter, after hacking into her school email account: *Yes, I would like to retake the test, Mr. Williams.* But it is always done with the best of intentions. Just like the time she DM'd Britney Spears to share how important it is to have solid girlfriends, or when she tried to backdoor her parents into a retirement community. A crafty problem solver with a knowing wink and a smile. You want Tess on your team in the last leg of a relay race because she will somehow always figure out how to bring home the win.

The essays on the following pages are the result of Tess's attempt to process an overwhelming pileup of events—an unexpected turn in a beloved career and the impending illness of a parent. I had a front row seat to her quickly turning these life changes into a movement, fueled with heart, absurdity, and soul. Tess has found humor, irony, and emotional resonance in the messiness of her life, while simultaneously being willing to expose her vulnerability, because that's who she is.

I hope that as you get to know Tess, you fall in love with her endearing ways and funny stories in the same way I have. Her tales are playful, all told through her unique and persuasive point of view. You will enjoy the ride, or I am sure she will convince you that you did. She can be very persuasive as evidenced by me writing this. See, she did it again.

Also, if there's any mention of me getting scared on a ropes course in Montana, I'm pretty sure I had COVID and that it never happened.

—Max Greenfield

We've Decided to Go in a Different Direction

Casting the Intern: Co-Star Billing

"Oh my God, I love your shoes. You know this dress would look so great with those."

That was my opening line when I worked as a salesperson at the clothing store BCBG, otherwise known as Bon Chic Bon Genre, which in French translates to "good style good attitude." This BCBG store was located in the trendiest part of LA's Sunset Boulevard, perfectly situated between Chin Chin and Le Petit Four—two very hot restaurants in 1999—making BCBG the crown jewel on the strip. I worked there part-time in college, and when I graduated, I bumped up my hours to full-time.

The store was magnificent in size and grandeur: two levels, with light-colored wood floors that complemented the neutral tone of the clothes featured each season. The brand was considered hot, and the vibe in the store was popping. High-energy fun combined with hard work. When it was slow, we would blast Janet Jackson and dance to "Rhythm Nation" in front of the mirrors—hands over faces, counting backward, "Five, four, three, two, one . . ." There was no TikTok so all our dance routines (and there were many) went undocumented. Probably for the best. There was always a lot of action, requiring no less than five salespeople, or in my mind dancers, for each shift.

I had the right disposition to work in retail. I was friendly and genuinely interested in other people. That's where I really honed my skills in striking up a conversation with just about anyone. Tourist, rushed executive, celebrity, mom needing a glow up . . . I could find a common thread with everyone. One time I helped three famous ladies—all close *FRIENDS* on and off camera—who were shopping together. They were so nice and appreciative to their smiley, overeager sales girl. They each purchased several items, maybe out of guilt, come to think of it now. They must have known I was working on commission. I go out of my way today to be overly nice to salespeople when I am retail shopping. Yes, girl, I see you and have been there.

Anyone who has ever worked in retail knows that you build a tight community with your co-workers because of all the hours you spend on the floor. Most of us were in our early twenties, navigating dating and trying to figure out our life goals and next steps. All my fellow salespeople considered the job a pit stop, not a destination, myself included. I had my sights set on becoming a casting director.

The idea of casting came naturally to me. If you've seen the movie *Up in the Air*, where George Clooney's character is a traveling human resources "fixer," so to speak, my dad had a very similar job. He was a management consultant for big, multimillion-dollar corporations and had to relocate often, which meant my family moved around a lot when I was a kid.

By twelfth grade, I had enrolled in seven different schools in three different regions of the country. I had the chance to start over with every new location and re-create myself, trying out different personas and casting the people who would be my friends, and later, my boyfriends. I became adept at reading people, at studying mannerisms and determining who would be a good match for me. I developed a keen eye for identifying different characteristics in people and negotiating what I was willing to change about myself to fit in. That skill of taking on different personas, combined with my love of theater and performers, expanded into an innate love for casting.

During an on-the-floor conversation about our aspirations in entertainment, I shared my professional ambition with a part-time salesgirl—think a young Maura Tierney from her *ER* days, a natural beauty with thick, dark, shoulder-length hair, perfect skin, and a raspy voice. I doubted "Maura," who was studying film at college and wanted to be a director, would stay long at BCBG. She possessed undistracted focus toward her future. Maura just felt like she was meant for bigger things, getting out and moving on up. One day, she excitedly told me she had just landed an internship with a movie director.

"Really? That's *so* cool. Would you possibly ask if the casting director working on the movie needs an intern?" I had no idea how to begin a career in casting, I had never even met a casting director, but I figured, why would anyone turn down free labor? Maura agreed to try to hook me up so I could get my foot in the door.

During our next shift together, Maura slipped me a piece of

paper with the name and phone number of the casting director working on the film. The following morning, I called and pitched myself for an intern position. The casting director must have sensed the overzealous (read: desperate) tone in my voice and taken pity on me, because she agreed to meet the next day at the Coffee Bean in Brentwood.

I left myself an hour and thirty minutes for the twenty-five-minute drive, blasting Tupac's "How Do U Want It" the whole way. Arriving ridiculously early, I found parking and sat in my car going over potential interview questions I might be asked. A lot of my television and media knowledge had been acquired in more recent years, because, growing up, we had not really been allowed to watch TV. (I know, I know . . . calm down, I found plenty of other ways to entertain myself.)

My parents encouraged my sister and me to read, play outdoors, ride bikes, explore the neighborhoods. And no, we weren't sequestered from pop culture like the Duggar family; it just was not how my parents wanted us to spend our free time. That said, I made up for lost time when I went to college and spent hours parked in front of a television (tuition money well spent).

About five minutes ahead of our scheduled meeting time, I took a deep breath, put my shoulders back, and walked inside to meet the casting director.

I spotted her right away. She had long, wavy dark hair, wire-rimmed glasses, and pale skin—very Anne Hathaway. I looked past the stack of scripts and papers on the café table in front of her and noticed she was wearing jeans. My immediate thought: *Oh no, I'm way overdressed*. I was wearing a blazer and some sort of dress pants . . . basically a suit. I thought that's what one was supposed to wear to a job interview. Little did I know that in the world of independent film, pajamas and dirty hair would have been acceptable. I looked like a recent graduate of a school of hospitality, applying to be a reservation specialist at the Marriott.

She looked up with a relaxed smile. "Hi, are you Tess?"

"Yes I am. Nice to meet you."

While I had zero casting experience to speak of, that didn't stop me from wielding all that I had learned and mastered working on the sales floor. Talking to strangers, disarming them, convincing them what they needed most. I chopped it up, broke it down, and convinced this woman why she had to hire me.

"I watch a lot of TV and go to the movies all the time," I told her.

"Who are your favorite actors?" she asked.

"Julia Louis-Dreyfus, Tom Cruise, Julia Roberts . . . I love your glasses, by the way."

"Oh, thank you! What's your schedule like?"

"My schedule is very flexible. If you need me to stay late, no problem. I am also very organized and take direction really well. I'm a quick study."

"So why do you want to work in casting?"

"I am fascinated by the process of picking who's right for which role. I did a fair share of theater growing up, but I consider myself a behind-the-scenes person. I like observing what makes a believable performance. I love actors." *Take a breath, Tess.*

Just as we wrapped up, she *hollywooded* me and let me know she was meeting *a few other candidates* for the internship and would call me when she settled on someone. I drove home with longing in my heart, replaying our conversation in my head. I really wanted this and was willing to work two jobs to make it happen. Three days later, she called. I had gotten the internship. Hello, Hollywood!

On my first day, I walked around the production office as if I were entering Disneyland for the very first time, wide-eyed, with a permanent smile. *Wait, are my dreams actually coming true?*

After giving me a quick tour of the office, "Anne," my boss, handed me a sheaf of papers. After introducing me to several other production assistants who were mulling around, "Anne," my boss, handed me a script and pointed to a folding table in the middle of the room and said, "Read this script first, then you'll move over to the bookcase to open these submissions." Okay on it. "Then sort headshots under the role the actor is being submitted for, and be sure to keep the agency submission letter. When you're done, alphabetize the agency letters." Yup, on it! At four thirty I was nearly finished, just when the mail arrived with—you guessed it—more manila envelopes. My hands were dry and cracked with several new paper cuts, but I couldn't care less. I was immersed. I would examine the headshot and cover letter from the agent, find the role on the huge bookcase, and place the headshot underneath the Post-it Note specifying the character's name. I loved it. I was blown away by the sheer quantity. There were at least five hundred headshots in the first batch. All these actors wanted to be in *this* movie. Wow, I must be working on one hot project. Back then there were no computer/online submissions like there are today; these were all submitted via regular US mail. The movie was titled *Race*, starring Paul Rodriguez as a local East Los Angeles resident running for city council.

Although I didn't get to see any actual auditions—those took place in the director's office—I was a sponge soaking up everything I could. Anne would return from her casting session, hand me a headshot, and politely request a Deal Memo and the SAG (Screen Actors Guild) contract be typed up. *Gulp.* Typed? Like on a typewriter? I was shown the blank forms and which information was to go where. Uh-huh, on it!

These contracts were the official agreement, and now *the SAG contracts were in my hands.* Back then—one thousand years ago—these contracts were three-ply carbon copies. One copy would be faxed to the agent, one would be given to the production assistant, and one would be left with the casting director to make the final cast list. So I had to insert this three-ply paper document carefully between the roller and the paper table of the typewriter, then turn the side knob clockwise to feed the paper in and set the carriage so I could begin typing in the blank space next to "Actor Name." I had never worked in an office, so I didn't know much about carbon copies, but one thing I did know was that there was no room for error. And my heart pounded with the responsibility I was entrusted with. Each key I pressed cut through all three sheets of paper.

Bottom line: If I made a mistake on these critical contracts containing vital information, there was no fixing it with a backspace, an eraser, Wite-Out, or any form of Liquid Paper. (Again, many of you probably have no idea what I'm talking about, since most of you have only seen a typewriter on the *The Crown*.) It had to be perfect, to the letter. If someone had a middle initial and I typed an *L* instead of a *K*, well, no paycheck, no credit. I would have to start over and throw out the botched contract. The guilt I still carry today about the amount of paper I wasted is chilling. I buried the contracts I screwed up deep in the trash. (Dear Environment, please forgive me, for I knew not the waste I made.) I started off slow and methodical, and with each passing day I became a better and more efficient typist. This movie had a lot of day players, also known as small speaking parts, so I got tons of practice. And Anne was a great boss—instructive and nice, no fluff, and all biz. She went on to win multiple Emmys for casting gigantic hits like *The West Wing* and *Mad Men*.

The casting internship with Anne lasted about four months, ending when the movie wrapped. I had become a little better versed on actors, agents, and process, but I was still a newbie, an outsider with no assurance this internship would even qualify me for another job, paid or unpaid. But I had to try. I had gotten a taste of casting and was now more determined than ever to build a career toward becoming a casting director.

I quit my job at BCBG and said au revoir to the steady paycheck. Per Anne's recommendation, I listed my internship on my résumé and faxed it to the Casting Society of America (CSA— you will often see those three letters following a casting director's name in TV and movie credits). It began as a guild of sorts for all casting directors, a centralized place for casting information and resources. Within one week of placing my résumé there as an "available casting assistant," a young male casting director plucked it from his pile of hopefuls and called me to set up an interview.

We met at Hugo's in West Hollywood, a bright and cheery place that served healthy breakfast dishes all day. He was sitting at a table in the back, and I sort of fell in love the moment I laid eyes on him. Think a John Early type, with perfectly styled blond hair, blue eyes, and a toothy smile. His look was preppy, like an '80s movie heartbreaker named Biff—pink Izod shirt collar *popped* and navy blue shorts with crisp white Stan Smith tennis shoes.

"John" told me about this new half-hour, multi-camera television pilot called *Desmond's Place* that had just been picked up as a series. He told me about the actors he had already cast as the series regulars, and about his casting office located on the Paramount lot. *Be still, my beating heart.* An actual movie studio lot that I had passed by hundreds of times. I was already envisioning the fantasy montage: driving through the famous gates, then me and John holding hands, skipping around the movie lot, both wearing the same denim jacket, laughing hysterically as we walked into our office, toasting our cosmos . . . until my reverie was interrupted by "So, do you have any questions?"

I retrieved a stack of three-by-five index cards from my purse. "Yes, as a matter of fact." I cleared my throat. "Where do you see your career in five years? How about ten?" Now that I was independently employed, I had to make sure I was hitching my wagon to someone on a trajectory toward long-term success. This would help me explain to my dad why quitting my job with health benefits was a good move. John smiled, clearly amused by my formality, and graciously tried to answer, but I can only imagine what he was really thinking. *Chill, girl, this is an assistant position—four hundred dollars a week before taxes, with zero security.*

After a little more chitchat, we stood to leave, and he handed me his business card. "Call me if you have any questions. I'm meeting with a few more candidates today, but I should know shortly."

I gazed into his blue eyes and thought, *You will be mine one day*, as if trying to telepathically will him to hire me. After the interview, I raced home to my small apartment just down the street, wrote a handwritten thank-you note, and drove to Kinko's to fax it. It seemed so modern and chic that he had an at-home fax machine! Who was this fancy casting dream boss?

Dear Mr. John Early,

Thank you for giving me the opportunity to interview to be your assistant. Your spin on the show is irresistible. Whatever I lack in experience, I will make up for it with a positive attitude and hard work. If you give me a chance, you will not regret it.

Sincerely,
Tess Sanchez

Thirsty AF, but it worked! At about six p.m. he called me and said, "I got your faxed note. I have a good feeling about you. I'm offering you the position." I was thrilled that he was willing to take a chance on me. This was a real paying job as a casting assistant on the Paramount Studios lot. That was my new title, and boy did I love hearing it that first day when John walked me around, introducing me to the series regular cast members led by Chi McBride.

Every morning I arrived around eight a.m., which in the entertainment industry is like 6:30 a.m. to the rest of the world. My desk was located in an area we referred to as "the pit." It was one main room where all the assistants had their desks and was flanked by the offices of four different casting directors all working on different projects.

I was so excited to get to know my fellow pit mates. They, however, did not share my desire to connect. On my first morning, I turned to my main suitemate—think Meg Stalter from *Hacks*, with a cool can't-be-bothered attitude—and said, "Hi, I'm Tess. I am John's new assistant. Who do you work for?"

"Meg" looked up from her papers and sized me up, then said in an exhausted tone, "I work for Lisa." Frigid welcome is an understatement. I could tell I was too eager and too green for her taste. She would roll in every day around nine a.m., shades on, singing some undetectable pop song, bags slung over each shoulder, holding a venti double frapp extra whip, with just enough room for a huge chip on her shoulder. Even though we were the same age, Meg had the confidence of a thirty-year vet, especially on the phone.

"Casting, this is Meg. Who is this? Yes, duh, I remember you. No, we haven't cast that role yet. Send in your submission and I will get it to her. No, Lisa isn't taking phone pitches. Send it in! Don't play that game with me, you know our address. Uh-huh, oh please, go tell your boss, I don't care, it's not going to get Lisa to return your call sooner. Later, bitch. No, you know I love you. Okay, goodbye. Bye, girl." Very cool.

We could all hear each other's business, and the actors would sit along the wall while they waited to be called, so they got to watch their own show of "the newbie and the vet." They could also hear the auditions that were happening on the other side of the door to any one of our bosses' offices.

When working on a television series, the smaller roles are called co-stars and the bigger roles are called guest stars. Co-star roles are usually a few lines. Agents will submit their less-experienced or new-to-the-business talent for these roles. As a casting assistant, I would call the agent and give an appointment time for their client to come audition for the role. Some days I would be invited to sit in on these auditions, listening to John give directions, making slight adjustments to an actor's performance. He would say, "Okay, that was good. Let's try it again, but this time pick up the pace." Listening to each of them read, I would try to anticipate what direction he would give next. Thus began my education in the art of the audition—the good, the bad, and the sweaty.

For the bigger guest star roles on an episode, like when Matt Damon guest starred on *Will & Grace*, the agent will pitch their client to the casting director, who (not requiring an actor of that level to audition) then calls the producers and says, "Matt Damon was pitched; he is available and loves the show. I think he would be great." Once approved, an offer is made to the agent. More often, that same process works in reverse, with the interest coming from a producer or director, and the casting director making the outgoing call with an offer to the agent, hoping the actor is a fan of the show.

My first big assignment was to compile a cast list with the actors' contact information. On Sunday nights, the script for that week's episode was delivered to each actor's home so they could prepare for the Monday morning table read. I spent an entire day formatting and updating this document before walking it over to the production office. Come Monday morning, when we arrived at the stage for the reading, the lead actress was angrily yelling at the director and several production assistants that she'd never received the script and couldn't possibly read it cold. My heart started to pound. *Why didn't she receive her script? I delivered the cast list with her home address included.*

Just then the production assistant pulled out the cast list and showed it to her, saying, "Isn't this your address?"

She replied with indignance, "I live at 1223 S. Stanley, *not* 1232 S. Stanley. Casting wrote the wrong address." Then she lifted her head and things started to move in slow motion as she narrowed her gaze and zeroed in on John.

Oh my God . . . it was my mistake. It was my first week on the job and I'd already royally fucked up. Was I going to be fired? Was John going to be fired? I opened my mouth to fess up, "It is my fau—" but John cut me off before I could finish.

"Christine, I am so sorry. This is a hundred percent my fault. I am making a note; I promise this won't happen again." He immediately disarmed her with his profuse apology and took the bullet for me.

I was embarrassed and upset that my mistake made him look bad. I felt as though I might throw up. The cast took their seats and read through the episode. As we got up to leave, John said, "Christine, you are incredible. That was truly hilarious."

She smiled and said in a showy, loud tone, "Thanks, doll," winking at him.

As we walked back to our office, I apologized to him immediately, assuring him that I would pay closer attention to detail. All he said was, "I know this won't happen again. Now let's move on."

Although I remained slightly nauseous for over a week, I never made that mistake again.

Another casting assistant duty was "checking avails" to see if an actor was available and interested in doing an episode by locating which agency the actor was represented by in this big book called the *Players' Guide* (yeah, this was still pre-internet). One afternoon I put a call in to Carmen Electra's agent to see if she was available for an episode of *Desmond's Place*. The assistant said, "No, she is shooting an MTV pilot," and promptly hung up.

"Wait, how long is she working on . . . ? Hello? Hello? Did he just hang up on me? Ugh, I have to call him back."

All of a sudden Meg slurped her frapp, infuriated, and said, "I have Carmen's dates, as well as Jenny McCarthy's availability.

Jason reps both!" she shouted, erupting in anger. "Please. Take the info. I cannot bear listening to you call him back. Consolidate and check a group of avails at each agency with one call."

The disdain that Meg had for me was palpable. She was consistently on the verge of losing her shit on me. It didn't help that her boss, Lisa, liked me and appreciated my cheery energy. Where Meg was nuts-and-bolts, fast with an encyclopedic knowledge of agents, actors, and phone numbers ready at the tip of her tongue, I was definitely behind on the learning curve. Over time my assistant skills became stronger, while I remained steadfast in my never-ending efforts to win Meg over.

On Friday nights, we would go from the office to the stage for the taping of the episode in front of a live studio audience. We would first stop by the dressing rooms and say hello to the guest star actors we had hired for the week. Then we would pop in to see the actors' agents and managers, who would be gathered in a small room off the stage with a video monitor to watch all the action onstage.

There was a buzzy connection between the audience and the actors, who were essentially doing live theater. My favorite part was always toward the end of the night, when the actors would get punchy and forget a line and start laughing. The audience would eat it up, as if they were in on the joke.

Being a part of all this, looking up at the packed risers filled with people laughing, I couldn't help but think, *I did it! Does it get any better?* My parents even made it to a taping of the show and sat in the audience. I was so proud to be milling around on the stage floor, waving up to them.

Thirteen episodes later the show was canceled, and I was on to the next gig, having gained a mentor in John and a casting credit as an assistant. I learned so much from John, and always appreciated that he was willing to take a chance on me. We remained very close, and my fantasy montage had come true ten times over. Together, we roamed the Paramount lot, toasted with our cosmopolitans, laughed, worked, even vacationed together.

One of my casting assistant temp jobs landed me working for Meg's old boss, Lisa. Having impressed Lisa, she went on to recommend me for an associate casting position, the next step up from assistant, for pilot season (January to May) at the Warner Bros. Network. At the time, the WB was the epicenter of young Hollywood. It was MTV and shows on the WB where all the young up-and-coming talent could be found. The key demo and target audience was women eighteen to thirty-five years old.

My meeting was with the grand dame, a casting queen well known for her eclectic style and incredible taste in talent—think Susan Sarandon, an East Coast transplant with a hint-of-Philly accent. Her reputation preceded her. Everyone told me she was tough. I was nervous—and a little surprised to find her warm and easy to talk to.

Her office smelled of patchouli, with stacks of papers and headshots scattered about a dark wood desk. Curated pieces of pottery and knickknacks with flea market panache lived in every nook and cranny. Joining my initial meeting with "Susan" was her number two, an up-and-coming protégé who was like a young Rosie Perez, having moved from Brooklyn for the job.

After the interview, as I was heading out, they handed me ten scripts. Susan's edict: "Make a list of actors you would cast in the main roles for each script, five to ten names for each role. I want to see what your taste is like. It's Friday, fax us your lists Monday morning, first thing."

"Yes, you got it." I walked out hugging the bundle of scripts to my chest.

My taste in actors? Huh? I stopped at a magazine stand on the way home and bought every teen mag I could find. Google didn't exist, and there was no IMDb (Internet Movie Database). Research on pop culture was based on lived experience, magazines, or walking the aisles of the closest Blockbuster Video for inspiration.

I read each script, wrote down the lead characters, and studied their descriptions. Two of the scripts I vividly remember were *Popular* written by Ryan Murphy and *Young Americans* written by Steve Antin; both scripts were packed with high-school-aged roles: aspirational social queens and hot boyfriend dreamboats. I paged through the magazines and compiled my wish list based on who represented the zeitgeist of the times in movies and television. I cast on my lists the likes of Julia Stiles, Jessica Alba, Kirsten Dunst, Jordana Brewster, Scarlett Johansson, and Kate Bosworth, along with Jason Priestley, Mark-Paul Gosselaar, Joey Lawrence, and Freddie Prinze Jr. The talent that was already on WB shows was Jessica Biel on *7th Heaven*, Alyssa Milano and Shannen Doherty on *Charmed*, and Sarah Michelle Gellar on *Buffy the Vampire Slayer*. On Sunday night I called a talent manager friend and read her the descriptions of each role, along with my casting wish list. She recommended I remove only one name who she felt played too old for the role. I made the change and faxed my lists on Monday morning, fingers crossed.

My choices made the cut. That afternoon I was offered the temp job. And so I left the world of being an independent freelance casting assistant to start my creative corporate education, with the goal of turning this temporary gig into a permanent one.

Susan had high expectations for her staff. I followed "Rosie's" lead and learned to keep my head down. Susan had a distinct tone to her voice when she was displeased, and she also had one of the greatest, most contagious laughs I'd ever heard. It would erupt from her office and could be heard reverberating down the hall. I worked diligently, making lists of actor ideas and checking avails with precision and efficiency. Sometimes I nailed it, and many times I didn't. "Good job!" was rarely uttered.

On any given day she would stand in her office, kick her leg out, and stretch until her hip popped. She wore baggy, draped clothing, clanging bracelets, several beaded necklaces, and a long scarf regardless of the season. As eccentric as she was, her razor-sharp eye for discovering young talent was undeniable.

Susan became even more legendary during the years I worked there, turning out stars like: Michelle Williams, Katie Holmes, Keri Russell, Scott Speedman, Jamie Foxx, Scott Foley, Penn Badgley, Jessica Biel, Sarah Paulson, Jennifer Garner, Alexis Bledel, Amanda Peet, Selma Blair, Joshua Jackson . . . and the list goes on. Rosie and I were lucky enough to meet many of them during Susan's general meetings with the actors. These were casual sit-downs to get to know the actor and their general backstory. The actors would rarely audition for a specific role during these meetings, but even still, they would be incredibly nervous in her presence. These meetings were more of a judgment of a person's charisma, a test of how captivating one was at small talk.

We met every up-and-comer the second their wheels touched down at LAX. In many cases, they would show up straight from the airport and leave their luggage in the lobby. When Susan decided that someone had that IT factor, the whole town listened. Every agent worked hard to get in her good graces with a steady stream of gifts, flowers, and wine delivered to her office. If she really liked you, she might even send an unknown actor directly to an agent's office to be considered for representation.

Susan found talent everywhere. I remember her getting a call from a manager who was out on his morning walk to get coffee and met a guy walking his dog. They got to talking; the manager thought this guy was oozing star magnetism, and soon learned that he was studying acting. One quick call to Susan and, later that afternoon, hunky dog walker/aspiring actor was sitting on Susan's couch. He went on to star on the WB show *Angel*. At this time in the business there was no social media, so you had to meet people and be willing to take some bets. Susan had a finely tuned radar and would sound the alarm when there was a hot ticket with potential.

After these meetings, Susan would occasionally say, "That girl is going to be a big star," or "Now HE is a star." I would wonder how she knew. In many cases she had not seen them perform or read a scene. It was just her gut, her supreme intuition, her more than ten thousand hours of experience. And guess what?

She was almost always right—Shia LaBeouf, Channing Tatum, Jessica Chastain, Amy Adams, to mention a few.

Corporate casting as a career provided me with structure and loads of creative thinking. Like an artist with a blank canvas, it's a challenge to make that painting feel harmonious. Character A is in love with Character B, who is related to Characters C and D. If one of the characters doesn't seamlessly fit in, the whole painting is thrown off. I loved the complexity and challenge of it.

It was a very exciting time for talent in the television landscape and in the entertainment industry overall, especially for the young actors living at the Oakwood Apartments, hoping to win their first big job. The furnished apartments on Barham Boulevard in Burbank, located next to Warner Bros., Universal, and Disney studios, also served as the backdrop to just about every *E! True Hollywood Story* about young stardom.

During the early aughts, there was urgency in the market and an immediacy to success and fame. Literally, it was here today, famous tomorrow. Everyone was intoxicated by the volume of opportunity and the pace at which things moved, from executives, to writers, to actors. Budgets were big and parties were even bigger, especially when it came to the annual New York Upfronts. Each television network would get one day to present their fall lineup of shows to advertisers, in the hopes of wooing them to buy on-air ad time, the networks with the most promising shows and biggest breakout stars being the most desirable to advertisers.

After the presentations, there used to be lavish, over-the-top parties for the buyers to rub elbows with the talent. Back then, entire casts were flown to New York to mingle with advertisers. And the WB Upfront parties were legendary. They were so hot, talent from other networks would show up. It was like a *Vanity Fair* party for twentysomethings. The Upfronts also initiated a shuffling of talent as new shows were ordered to series and others were canceled. There would always be a flurry of phone calls seeking information about what talent was returning, who was newly available, what was possible . . .

The young writers walking our halls who were creating shows for the WB Network and shepherding their projects from pitch to final casting choice were the likes of Ryan Murphy, Greg Berlanti, J. J. Abrams, Max Mutchnick, Mindy Kaling, Darren Star, Jason Katims, Kevin Williamson, and Amy Sherman-Palladino, just to name a few. And yes, a twenty-eight-year-old Ryan Murphy pitching a show was just as supremely charismatic then as he is today. He was a straight-up visionary, long before *Nip/Tuck*. When he pitched a show, execs sat riveted with checkbook in hand. The WB was a creative wonderland filled with iconic television producers of tomorrow, most of whom I would work with again in the years to come as they built their media empires.

Susan's office was where we held the official "network test," the last audition for the final cast selection. No additional hoops to jump through, this was it. Usually, there were two or three actors up for one role, all nervously waiting in the lobby before being called in for their read. I had to pinch myself that I was actually there—albeit invisible, squeezed in the back corner, perched on a credenza, holding my breath.

After watching three different actors read the same material,

Susan would turn to the network president and say, "What did you think?" Fifteen people sat in silence as she commanded the room; tensions were always high. Oftentimes, the president would defer to her, saying, "Who did *you* like?"

The producers had their first choice in mind and then it was time for them to defend and advocate, and hopefully Susan agreed. When it was a slam dunk and everyone was on the same page, Susan would sometimes call an actor back into the room after their audition and tell them they got the part on the spot. We would see tears of joy as their knees buckled in euphoric excitement and relief. It was absolutely exhilarating to watch people's lives at the precipice of stardom, their dreams being realized.

On the flip side, when the actors fell flat or no consensus was reached, the air in the room would get thick. I dreaded the conversation that would ensue: "Who else is out there? Which actor could be a better fit?" Twelve executives, a director, studio heads all firing off questions, with multiple side conversations taking over pockets of the room: "Did Simon Rex read for this role?" or "Did Selma Blair go on tape yet?" I would sit there praying I had all the information they needed at my fingertips.

"Tess, did you get Kate Bosworth to go in to read or did she tape in New York?" Susan would ask.

With my heart pounding in my chest I'd answer, hoping to sound confident. "She is shooting a movie in Hawaii until April fifteenth and cannot read the script while on location."

Other times Susan would insist we have the actor come back into the room and read the scene again after the director stepped out to give some notes. You just could never predict the outcome of those network tests. Anything could and did happen.

After I had survived my temp casting associate position for the five months of pilot season, Susan casually walked by my desk one day, and with no detectable enthusiasm declared: "Tess, yeah so, you're going to stay. I'm giving you a three-year contract," and just kept walking past my desk. Her distinct casual cadence almost sounded like she was in conversation with herself.

"Okay! Thank you?" I said to the back of her head.

However, despite the news of being offered a contracted position, my insecurities were still nagging on the inside, and each day I was challenged to find my confidence and sense of belonging. *Did I really deserve to be here?* I tried to project ease in every situation but couldn't help feeling I would be asked to leave at any moment. With a promise of more permanence, this contract quelled my inner voice for a moment, but that voice slowly crept back into rotation.

2

Red Wool Beanie:
Shared Card

Dating in Hollywood before texting existed seems nearly impossible, right? Allow me to set the scene: It was the early 2000s, more of a flip phone and BlackBerry kind of world. My career was on track, and my romantic mindset was, in casting terms, *tech avail and interested* (actors without existing contractual obligations, who have heard about a project and are interested in engaging). I was single and interested in mingling with all types of suitors.

Let's just get this out there: I was never good at casual dating. If I liked someone, I usually REALLY liked them. There was no shortage of cute guys; I was surrounded by a bevy of artistic up-and-comers. It was the heyday of workplace romance. Every agency mailroom, power agent's desk, and TV executive assistant pool was the setting for the romantic origin stories of more couples than I can count. Something about being in the trenches and working long hours made for a natural mating ground.

I had been dating (on and off) a successful TV writer—think a twenty-seven-year-old Topher Grace. Not a showstopper (sorry, Topher), but he had style and swag. He was smart, outrageously witty, and always just out of reach. He had perfectly mastered that slightly aloof, *I-am-so-busy-and-in-demand* thing, which was annoying because (a) that was my usual play, and (b) I hated that it was working on me. I could not believe he was not proclaiming his love for me. And embarrassing as it is to admit, his unattainability kept me on the hook and coming back for more.

"Topher" would call my home phone and say, "Hey, we should get together tonight" (always on the day of), to which I would nonchalantly say, "Yeah, I think I can make that work," and then scramble to change my existing plans. We had very good sexual chemistry. I really loved our nights together. We would meet at the Chateau Marmont, or whatever the latest hot spot was, talk for hours, have cocktails, laugh, then go back to his house and you-know-what to Coldplay.

He was successful enough to have already bought his first home, a sexy bachelor pad in the Hollywood Hills, although I never saw it in the daylight (pathetic, I know). This dance went on for much longer than it should have, almost a year—okay, a full year . . . fine, well over a year. I was sure any day he was going to turn around and say, "What have I been doing all this time? Of course I am madly in love with you." (Please hold for laughter from the studio audience.)

I finally reached my breaking point when I invited Topher to visit my parents, who were in England at the time. Unwilling to take my invitation seriously, he laughed it off whenever I brought it up. It became clear, despite how long this affair had been going on, that I was nothing more than a regular booty call. He did not want to take the relationship to the next level. I was in love with the *potential* of a relationship with him, but as my mom would say, his taxi light was not on. It was time to say adios to Topher.

And while you might judge me for hanging around well beyond the relationship expiration date, for the record, *I* broke it off. I'll take the win where I can get it.

After a Christmas vacation spent with my parents, I was back in Los Angeles, ready to start 2003 in new digs, newly single. I headed out with my girls—think Meagan Good, Jessica Biel, and Selena Gomez. I would be JLo (yeah, I get it, I wish) in her *In Living Color* era, the look being more Jenny the funky fly girl.

It was a Saturday night on the Cahuenga Corridor, a new up-and-coming hot strip of bars and restaurants lining both sides of Cahuenga Boulevard. We were out for a quick bite, then to a bar called Nacional. We'd landed a few seats in the corner when I looked across the room and locked eyes with a guy. And when I say "locked," it was like a science fiction movie where a tractor beam of light connected us. I was jolted down to my toes.

My friends and I continued to gab until "Jessica" asked, "Who's that guy staring at you?" I replied that I didn't know, but I was officially tech avail, so I smiled and waved him over. With Jay-Z's "Big Pimpin'" playing in the background, he made his way over from the bar in his jeans, white T-shirt, and red wool beanie, with the biggest smile on his face, free of any restraint. He clocked me with his warm, welcoming eyes and said, "Hi, I'm Max," in a raspy, deep, cigarette-singed voice.

I looked up at him and said, "Hi, I'm Tess. Have we met before? What do you do?"

He responded with just a bit of importance, "I'm an actor. I recently moved here from New York." His accent also gave him away. In my head I thought, *Noooo, not an actor. Be anything, just not an actor.* But the immediate and palpable chemistry between us quickly erased my hesitation over his chosen profession. I asked if I could see his hat. He took it off and out flopped this thick, wavy black hair. *Hmm . . . yes, this will do.*

As the night wore on, we continued our small talk, and each of our respective groups of friends faded away until I insisted that we go and find them. Max agreed but asked for my phone number first, and I obliged. He then said, "Don't leave without saying goodbye." I caught up with my friends just as they were heading out, so I didn't have a chance to find Max. Yes, I was intrigued, but he was an *actor.* Besides, he had my number . . . *if he calls, he calls,* I told myself.

As I walked in my door that night, my phone was ringing. I picked it up.

"Hello?"

"Hey, this is Max. You left without saying goodbye." I smiled. "Can I come by and say good night to you?"

Hmmm, is this guy going to chop me up into pieces? As polite as I could muster at 1:40 a.m., I answered, "Oh, I don't think so. It's pretty late."

"I won't even stay five minutes. I just want to see you," he persisted.

In hindsight, maybe it was not the smartest idea, but for

some reason I agreed. At least if I was murdered by this guy, they could trace my last phone call back to him. No less than ten minutes later, I heard a knock on my door. When I opened it, there was Max. We stood there, looking into each other's eyes, smiling. And there it was again, that sci-fi lightning bolt connecting us.

"Well?" I finally said to cut the tension.

Then he went in for the kiss. A perfect, showstopping, drop-your-glass kiss, with a jolt of electricity so intense between us, I am pretty sure we lit up the entire solar system the second our lips touched. It rendered me speechless.

Max pulled away and said, "Now *that's* how you say good night!" As he stepped back, he took off his red wool beanie and handed it to me. My thoughts were a jumble: *What's this for? A souvenir?* I remained quiet while he turned on his heel to walk back to his car. I knew I looked confused.

Looking over his shoulder with the confidence of Ryan Gosling, he shrugged and said, "I guess you *have* to see me again . . . you have my hat." And with that, he got back into his car and drove away. True to his word, this all went down in the span of five minutes. *Well*, I thought, *that was something. What the actual fuck?*

Max called me on Monday, and I returned his call the following day. We met up for our first date at a bar called the Well, after a comedy showcase I had attended. I was dressed "corporate cute" in jeans, a blazer, and boots. And he was in basic LA actor uniform: baggy jeans and a plaid flannel shirt. This bar was low-lit, no loud music, no friends, no distractions to muddle my perspective. We settled in and began to talk . . . and talk . . .

and talk. Max explained he was a dramatic film actor, edgy and brooding, and not interested in TV.

My initial reaction to this: (1) Pardon *moi* while I barf, and (2) Perfect! Our professional lives will never intersect because I work in the shallow land of television, and I love it! *Come on, guy!* Although in his defense, television back then was certainly not a fraction of what it is today. Shows like *Ozark* or *The Handmaid's Tale* did not exist yet. It was all network cop crime shows and medical shows for the dramatic types. There was a clear dividing line between television and film actors, and they didn't cross over. And if you were on TV, that was it, there were no sexy movies in your future.

Max, like so many young actors, didn't yet know how to define himself as an artist. He thought he was Matt Dillon from *The Outsiders*. Little did he know that in about a decade, after thousands of auditions and a thousand disappointments, he would morph into America's TV clown, Schmidt, on the hit show *New Girl*. And that clown would be nominated for an Emmy and a Golden Globe for his comedic performance on *television*.

We talked about our ambitions, our friends, our families. I remember being struck by his ease. He would gaze at me, smiling, riveted. This adoration didn't feel warranted. Maybe I was just jaded after dating guys whose eyes glazed over whenever they heard a woman's voice. Max would tilt his head and really listen. He was inquisitive and engaged, and so very present. He was the personification of charisma: brain, lungs, heart, and gobs upon gobs of charm.

We sat and talked for over three hours. His thick accent

grew on me, and I actually found it endearing. (Fun fact: Max eventually had to hire a dialect coach to rid him of his regional sound. Yes, it was that thick.) I learned about his friends back home in "Dobbs" (Dobbs Ferry), who all had traditional mob nicknames and referred to their mothers as "Ma!" And he listened intently as I told him about my family and aspirations to further my career in casting. More importantly, I learned we were both at the same station in life, working toward something bigger. Neither of us had connections in Hollywood, just vision and passion in pursuit of our dreams.

It felt comfortable and easy talking with him, but it was also exciting, sexy, and a little dangerous. I had never met anyone like him before. He felt like a city kid, with a knowingness about him. He knew a lot about art and music, which in my West Coast dating life, was new. He asked me who my favorite artist was. I said, "It changes, but right now I am really into Chuck Close." Max responded with, "He is one of my favorites," and referenced his early self-portraits.

Later that night, as he walked me to my car, he told me he had something for me and stopped by his car to grab it. It was a mixed CD he had made for me. As I popped it in the CD player in my car with the door open to hear a sample, Max lit up a hand-rolled cigarette and pulled in a deep drag. Then, without an ounce of inhibition, began to sing full-out one of the Rolling Stones' songs, "Beast of Burden." It wasn't like his voice was that impressive, but he just had this spontaneous freedom to him. After dating self-important guys who took themselves so seriously, I found this unabashed guy refreshing. I was intrigued and amused that he was so comfortable being himself. I liked being around that kind of energy and wanted more of it.

The mix had carefully curated songs from the Cure, Nick Drake, some Zeppelin, the Rolling Stones, Mazzy Star—all hot and brooding, just like him. (I still have the CD, though I no longer possess anything on which to play it.) We left that night, making plans for the upcoming weekend. Max insisted that he pick me up and take me on a real date: dinner at his favorite restaurant.

That Saturday night, we drove to Cafe Stella in his black Pathfinder. He had thoughtfully gifted me with a book of Chuck Close's works. It was exactly one week after we met that we began our inseparable path together, and exactly two weeks after meeting that we slept together. As we lay in my bed, sheets wrapped around us, I thought, *Okay, sooo, what happens next? Should I invite him to spend the night?* As I was deliberating, Max pulled me into his arms, and in less than one minute he was asleep. Out cold. He was so comfortable, so relaxed, it didn't even occur to him to leave. I lay awake marveling at his ease, until I eventually fell asleep with his arms still wrapped around me.

In the morning, I awoke before him to my phone ringing. It was my girlfriend Jessica. "Oh, hey girl, we're out front. Remember, we're going to the salt scrub spa." Oops, I had forgotten. I spoke a little louder to wake the super sleeper. "Give me ten minutes and I'll be out there." Max didn't stir, so I lightly tapped his shoulder. "Hey, I forgot I have a spa day with my friends."

He opened his eyes, and with his huge smile said, "Good morning." He looked so well-rested. As he popped out of bed with no clothes on, I finally got a real look at this person in the bright morning light. And the first thought that crossed my mind was *Powder*, that movie about the super pale guy. It was February, winter in LA, and I had never in my life seen skin so white, almost translucent.

Being of Mexican descent, I have olive skin. I don't sunburn. If I walk to my car across a grocery store parking lot, I'll be three shades darker by the time I get there. Not this guy. As he turned around, I saw a solar system of little chocolate-chip moles all over his back. Didn't see that coming.

I know it sounds shallow, but I did have some concerns. *Who is this pasty, hairless, chocolate-chip man who sleeps so soundly for ten straight hours in a stranger's bed that he needs to be* woken up *in the morning*? I got over all that quite fast.

We set sail on our relationship, never needing to discuss being exclusive, because we were always together—every single night. It was effortless, devoid of games and miscommunications. *So, this is what people mean when they say it should be easy and uncomplicated*, I thought. We met each other's friends, each other's parents, and fell madly in love in a short time.

My senses were so heightened by the love endorphins I was producing, that even the air felt different on my skin. Max confessed one night, less than three months in, that he had fallen in love with me. I felt his love and I was mesmerized on a cellular level. To be the object of his affection felt like a ray of sunshine surrounding me in a warm embrace every day. It was otherworldly. We were merely passengers on a boat that had a predestined course.

Our courtship was blissful, with a lot of late nights, sexy dinners, bottles of wine, parties, cocktails, and more bottles of wine. I didn't pay much attention to what we were drinking and how much. We hosted many parties at my apartment, which he had moved into after four months. Artists, actors, photographers, and writers were always around and welcome. It felt appropriate for our twenties, and I can't deny the intoxicating creative energy that surrounded us. We were everywhere, and the center of the party.

But those days had to come to end; it just wasn't sustainable, especially as my workload got heavier and I didn't have the time to meet up with Max after work. After about eighteen months of nonstop late nights, our lifestyles began to clash. I would get home after a long day and just want to chill and watch a movie, and he would already be out with friends and wouldn't come back until two a.m. On other nights, I would turn in early and wake up to find Max passed out on the couch with all the lights on and our record player skipping on the last song of an album. We would agree to stay in together, but come ten p.m., he would justify "a quick drink, just down the street, for an hour," which it never was. It was gradual, but I noticed the widening gap as his nights out and my nights in became more frequent. The fun, if that is what you want to call it, did not outweigh my desire for career success. Nothing was going to jeopardize the road I had been on for the last four years.

In the fall of 2005, Max told me that he had decided to rent a loft down the street, because he felt like I was annoyed when he was out late so often with his friends (which I most definitely was). *I'm sorry . . . a what?!* I should have just cut ties at that exact moment, but I was too close to have any kind of perspective, and he was *really* selling it. He said that we could both have keys and that he could paint there during the day (he was doing a lot of painting at the time), or if he was going out, he could crash there and not disturb me. Okay, I was listening. He said he would be getting the keys in the next day or so, and when he did, he called me at work to come and meet him at *our* artist's loft.

When I arrived, I found that over the course of just two days, he had furnished it with a couch, a chair, and a bed. Wow, that was fast for someone who "just came up with the idea." I went along with the new arrangement, but it was not long before he was spending almost all his time down at *our loft*. "Hey, I'm down here painting, so I think I'll just stay here tonight." He was pulling away and did not know how to do it swiftly or humanely, so he continued to kill our relationship little by little. Death by a thousand paper cuts.

There were always people in the background when he called, and I suspected a lot of drinking was happening, and that became something I tried to negotiate with him. It turned into three, four, then five nights a week that we would spend apart. I know you're thinking, *Girl, wake up!* It was confusing, though; we were so entangled emotionally. We were inseparable for two and a half years, and the pulling away was bewildering.

Max and I had a trip planned, departing on December 26 for a week together in Mexico. Tickets were paid for, hotel booked. I was hoping this was going to be the thing to get us back on track. Then Max called on December 16 to say, "Hey." Everybody knows nothing good starts with the word "hey."

I mentioned that we hadn't seen each other in almost a week. "What's going on? Everything okay?"

Finally, he mumbled, "I can't do this anymore. I want to do my own thing."

I stood there, heart in my throat.

"Okay, well, what about the trip?"

"I can't," he said.

I hung up, daggers puncturing my chest. I was crushed. But I was also a little bit relieved. There was no more wondering or trying to manage this once beautiful thing that had become so frayed. I couldn't appreciate this yet, but Max had shown me what was possible; he had introduced me to real intimacy. This connection had been life-changing. If this was over, at least I knew what it felt like to be truly seen and cherished by someone for who I was, not for who they wanted me to be.

But in that moment I was numb. There was so much I didn't know or understand about what was really going on with him. I remember calling my dad and saying, "This hurts every part of me, and it feels like I will always feel this way." He explained that grief takes time—it will come and go and come back again, until the days when it hurts less will come more often.

On December 26, I boarded that flight to Mexico by myself. I ordered a glass of champagne and slowly sipped it as tears streamed down my face onto the armrest of the empty seat next to me. I had never been on a trip by myself, but staying in LA was not an option. I had told a few friends, but I was not yet ready to talk about the breakup. I had never been broken up with, I had always done the breaking. Now I was in survival mode; my heart cracked in half.

I arrived in Puerto Vallarta and checked into the hotel: a suite for two, now just one. After getting settled and unpacking my things, my phone rang—it was none other than my old boss John. "Where are you?" he said.

"I'm at my hotel," I said.

"Oh, really? The one with the fountain in the middle?"

"Yes, why?"

"Open your hotel door and look down into the atrium."

I opened the door and moved to the railing overlooking the fountain; there before me were a gaggle of my gay besties, waving and hollering, John standing in the middle. "Girl, get your ass down here immediately!" I knew they were going to be in the same city, but I had no idea they would be within walking distance of my hotel, and certainly had no expectation of seeing them.

I laughed and ran downstairs to jump into their arms. I spent the next eight days embraced and celebrated by my loyal, pretty, happy, fun, gay brigade—wall-to-wall gays who treated me like a queen. It was how Tess got her groove back . . . with a little help from a Brazilian soccer player with gorgeous, muscled thighs. As I made out with Carlos in the moonlight on the beach, I had tears in my eyes with the lingering sadness of losing Max and moving on. And this sweet guy brushed the hair out of my face and said ever so sweetly in a Portuguese accent, "Whoever let you go, Tess? You are um tesouro." While

I had not gotten my groove all the way back, this did help the process along.

Meanwhile, back in LA, Max got his wish. He was alone in that sparse, dark loft with its concrete walls and floors, where he proceeded to drink himself into oblivion. The drinking led to other things, as it often does, and the isolation and the loneliness fed the beast even more. While I was surrounded by friends who were building me back up, brick by brick, Max was having a very different experience. I chose at that time and even today not to dig too deeply into the details of what happened during that period when we weren't speaking, but I heard it was dark and destructive. A blur of unsavory people in and out, taking advantage of Max as he slipped further away into the tight grip of addiction.

Our paths did eventually cross after two and a half months, and what I'd heard was true—he was messy, thin, and even paler than usual. I smiled with concern, and he smiled back as we spotted each other across La Poubelle, a moody French restaurant in Beachwood Canyon that we had frequented in the past. I stood with confidence as he approached. He opened his arms to give me a tight, lingering hug. As his eyes locked on mine, there was deep sadness in his gaze; I could see how broken he was. I looked away and told him I had to go, leaving a million things unsaid.

He asked if he could call me, and despite my better judgment, I nodded yes, mostly because I did not feel like I had closure with how abruptly things had ended. Although the last eight months of our relationship found us slowly drifting apart, and even though we'd been broken up these past couple of months, I didn't feel done yet.

We began talking on the phone maybe once a week for a few weeks, keeping the conversations light because neither of us was ready to delve deeper into the complicated break. Eventually he asked if we could go to dinner. Half of me knew this was not a good idea, but it was the other half of me that agreed. Seeing him in this fractured state was tough. I felt his pull and his need. *Well, hello, Al-Anon. We have an emergency.* I didn't know what I was looking at exactly. I had never been around an addict.

We said goodbye that night after our dinner, and I went home to bed. I didn't know, or care to ask, where he was going; it was not home, that was for sure. But at four thirty in the morning, every phone in my house was ringing. I finally picked up.

"Hello."

"Hey, it's me."

"Is everything okay?"

"No, not really."

"What's going on?"

"I think . . . I think I might be dying."

There was a somberness and quiet to his confession. Then, sitting straight up in bed, I said, "Where are you?"

"I'm standing at your front door," he answered.

I walked upstairs, opened the door, and there was Max, looking hollow-eyed, frail, and intensely scared. I let him in and put him in the bathtub. I don't know why; I must have seen that in a movie or something. There was no talking. Afterward, I remained with him until he fell asleep.

When he woke up around midday, he said, "Thank you," and hugged me. "I'm going to go. I need help."

That very Saturday, in March 2006, Max checked into a rehab center to be treated for his addiction to drugs and alcohol, and he has been sober ever since.

We were not married, not even together, and still we found our way back to each other. He asked me to visit him in rehab, which I did. Those conversations were heavy and often hard, but we developed a deeper bond, with no promise of anything more than what we had right then. And slowly I allowed him back into my life. My parents and friends were apprehensive about the rekindling, but I did not care. I could tell by being around him he was seriously motivated and profoundly different. And so we began again.

Max's intentions never wavered. He was very clear that he wanted to remain sober and he wanted me in his life. At this time, staying sober meant, first and foremost, being of service to the program he was working. He approached his sobriety with earnest and honest humility, going to meetings every day at seven a.m. and sweeping the floors of meeting halls. In order to prove his commitment to me, he made daily amends, showing up for me like he once had. He was rebuilding trust with his words and actions, being in sync, and performing small acts of kindness. He had gone missing from his life for what felt like a very long time. I had almost forgotten that magical person I first met. Now that he was clean, the initial light that once glowed in and around him had returned. There was no greater feeling than being enveloped by that light when in his presence. His eyes were clear, and his heart was so full of gratitude. We celebrated each other's small victories and supported one another through struggles. Our life together was headed in a new direction.

That chance meeting and sliding-door moment on the Cahuenga Corridor in 2003 was twenty years ago. Our deeply rooted foundation is uncomplicated. We fell in love as equals, without pretense or agenda. It was simple and undeniable.

Today our lives are more complicated and busier, but that initial spark remains. Max at his core is the same person I met, not as hot and brooding, but just as kind and a whole hell of a lot funnier, which I often like to take credit for. And he loves me a lot. Like, *a lot* a lot. And for that, I am grateful.

3

Casting:
The Big Leagues

If Susan, my boss at the WB, was the queen of casting, then I was the Tony Hale to her Julia Louis-Dreyfus on *Veep*. While I did not hold her purse for her, I didn't sit until she was comfortably seated first, I never shared my opinion with other executives without her prior approval, and my schedule was 100 percent dictated by her schedule—I ate lunch when she ate lunch—and I joined in on conversations only when invited. Boundaries were made crystal clear about speaking out of turn. It sounded like this:

"That question was directed to me, not you."

"I'm sorry, understood, it won't—"

Cutting me off, she would then say, "Can you close the door behind you? I need to make a call."

I would turn with my head hung low and skulk back to my desk, mumbling to myself the whole way.

When I saw my phone light up with Susan's extension, my heart would race, as I tried to anticipate the reason for her call.

"Hello?"

"Tess, did you check on Milo's availability? Remember I asked you on Monday to find out and get him to audition for the Untitled Palladino Project."

"Yes, I called. They said he would read for interest."

"Why didn't you tell me that?"

"I'm sorry, I just found out like twenty minutes ago."

"How long ago? It is Tuesday. Why did it take you from yesterday until now to get this information? When I ask you to do something, I don't want to chase you down. Don't let this happen again!" *Click.*

"Understood— Hello?"

FUCK. Urgency always, Tess. Get the goddamn info.

Another of her pet peeves, besides tardy information, was misspelling an actor's name. I would hand her a list of ideas for a role, and she would hand it back to me like a teacher, with red ink circling every misspelled name: "MAKE CORRECTIONS." I am a terrible speller, and even today rely heavily on Google and Siri. I worked so hard to deliver on her expectations, and often worried that she regretted hiring me.

After she promoted me to manager of casting, under my new contract I received a company cell phone—BlackBerry— and my very own personalized stationery and business cards. I was legit, baby! I placed two business cards in a neatly folded piece of letterhead and sent them to my parents. I knew they would be so tickled. If you walked by me in Ralphs (an LA supermarket), I would likely hand you a business card. I doled them out like candy. I might have even given one to my dry cleaner in West Hollywood.

With my new credentials in tow, I was sent on my first scouting trip to San Antonio, Texas, to cover the Latino Comedy Festival. It was hosted by then-newcomer from *That '70s Show*, Wilmer Valderrama. I would take thorough notes during the comics' sets and then race up to my hotel room to call Susan and report back on which acts I saw.

I sat on the edge of my hotel room bed, officiously rattling off details about each performance. Listening to my meticulous notes, she would sound bored. "Yeah, go on. Yeah, I know him; he's not funny. Oh, George Lopez, yeah, I know him; he's been around forever." Each phone call was a total test of my confidence, which would dwindle away until she'd stop the conversation and say, "Hey, I have to go. Call me later." *Click*.

"Oh, okay," I would say to no one on the other end of the line, then think to myself: *I bored her straight off the phone*. The pressure I put on myself that first trip was staggering. Based on her lackluster responses when I pitched known entities, versus the interest she expressed in finding new, original voices, I began to better understand my mission: discovering new talent with the potential to be breakout stars, not those whom she considered already discovered and circling the track. What got her excited was the hunt and the discovery. It was trial by fire. There was no handbook or guide, and she certainly didn't spell anything out.

Everything I absorbed came from observation. I also learned how to bullet point the highlights and regulate my passion for when it really mattered. I had to select the people I was going to get behind and provide evidence as to why. Saying someone was hilarious was not going to cut it. I was being paid for my perspective, and Susan entrusted me to be her eyes and ears on the ground. I exhausted every venue, every show, determined to find a kernel of original talent if it killed me.

After that assignment, I was sent to cover the US Comedy Arts Festival in Aspen, the country's premiere comedy event. This was during a time in the business when a comedian would perform at the new faces show, and a bidding war would start between networks and studios the minute they walked off the stage. It was thrilling, and deals would move at lightning speed. Comedians would arrive at the festival virtually unknown and leave with a six-figure development deal with a major broadcast or cable network.

During these annual trips, I developed my comedic taste by watching seasoned comedians perform a range of styles, and I learned to pinpoint perspectives that would be funny for a broad audience. Which comedians were incredible storytellers? Which of the talent were better writers than performers? Who had charisma onstage but had not figured out who they were as a stand-up yet? Was there a seed of talent indicating who would become the next Ray Romano, Jerry Seinfeld, Kevin James, or Ellen DeGeneres?

Multi-camera sitcoms were thriving at the time, with loads of opportunity, high stakes, and big wins. I was thrilled when the Aspen Comedy Festival asked me to join their Board of Directors. Then I started covering Chicago's Second City (home of many an *SNL* alum) and the Just for Laughs festival in Montreal. It was exhilarating to be one discovery away from changing the course of someone's life, or at least that's how it felt at the time.

One of my early passion projects was a sketch show from a Chicago-based comedy troupe called For the Kids. I saw them dozens of times in Los Angeles and finally helped them land a spot in the Aspen Comedy Festival, which eventually led to a development deal with the WB Network. To have endorsed their show and seen it embraced by these talented comedy executives was a proud early accomplishment while working for Susan; it at once fueled my passion and validated my scouting efforts. Sort of.

There was no celebration. The general attitude from the higher-ups was: *You don't get accolades for doing your job. Does an airline pilot deserve accolades every time they land a plane? No, that is their job. This is yours. Keep your foot on the gas. Now, what's next?* I remained humble.

You could find me three to four nights a week at the Improv, Laugh Factory, Comedy Store, Largo, Second City, Upright Citizens Brigade, or the Groundlings. I would walk in, avoid the waitress (no money for drinks), and start taking notes. No one paid me overtime or reimbursed me for gas. I was dogged in my pursuit to expand my understanding of this world and the players in it. And I met some of my favorite performers, even now.

I saw newcomer and writing phenom Mindy Kaling's show *Matt & Ben*. She owned the stage with undeniable confidence, as if she had been there her whole life. Shortly thereafter she wrote and produced her pilot about her real-life best friend titled *Mindy and Brenda* at the WB. Another one of my favorite shows was Casey Wilson and June Diane Raphael's *Rode Hard and Put Away Wet*. I was so impressed with their ballsy writing and no-holds-barred performance that I ran up to introduce myself right after they got off stage. As the ever-the-cool comedy girls, they greeted me with a relaxed gracious star power. Subtext . . . *calm down, girl.* I was like no, you don't get it, *pant, pant, pant* you are never getting rid of me. True to my word since that day I have hounded their agents, and stalked their availability for numerous projects over the years. And yes I have offered and begged on more than one occasion. I got to know Fred Armisen as a drummer playing his character Fericito, which he would end up playing on *SNL*, and Will Forte as a spray-painted silver statue along with Melissa McCarthy ruling the stage at the Groundlings, Craig Robinson playing the keys, Seth Meyers doing a show called *Pick-Ups and Hiccups*. I watched and got to know a young Kevin Hart, who had the same amount of swag then that he has today. I spent many nights at Largo on Fairfax Avenue, the premiere alternative-comedy place to be, watching Sarah Silverman, Zach Galifianakis, and Patton Oswalt among many others.

I loved this world. Later, as Max folded into my life, he would come with me some nights, and we would break down the sets afterward. Most of the time, we agreed . . . but hey, what did this guy really know about comedy? I was the expert. One night there was an open mic at the Comedy Store, and Max—unknown at the time—went up onstage to try his hand at stand-up with some material about khaki pants. It was disastrous, devoid of punch lines, and lacking any comedic observations. Oh, Maxie . . . no, honey.

If I had that ten-minute set on tape today, I would use it as an instructional video to demonstrate what having no comedic point of view looks like. What so many gifted stand-ups make look so easy, is not easy at all, and takes years to master. I applaud Max's fearlessness but am glad he was one and done.

During my years at the WB Network, I experienced for the second time what it meant to have a work family. If Susan was the mother I was desperate to impress, I set my sights on a six-foot-four, Kentucky-raised man who ran the unscripted division to be my work husband—think a gay Vince Vaughn with a deep voice and southern drawl. Everyone was in love with this tall drink of water. He was magnetic.

"Vince" introduced me to his close-knit group of friends, who soon became my posse. I was his plus-one to almost everything, and he was mine. He developed a show called *The Surreal Life*, putting a group of celebrities looking to make a comeback in one house together, including Flavor Flav, Verne Troyer, Vanilla Ice, and Brigitte Nielsen. And my other favorite, *Beauty and the Geek*, produced by Ashton Kutcher, which matched up nerds with beauties in competitive challenges in hopes that sparks would fly. Today, the unscripted genre is fully realized, as hits like *Love Is Blind*, *America's Got Talent*, and the Real Housewives franchise dominate ratings and online chatter. But these shows were buzz-worthy and in the zeitgeist even without social media to help boost ratings.

My older sister and mentor at the office was an Amanda Peet type, the wise, smart, funny, tightly wound co-head of Drama Development. She always had my back, was witness to my growing pains under Susan, and applauded my ascension through the ranks. Amanda was and still is a true ally, an early example of a woman reaching down to pull me up.

I was given this incredible opportunity to find and develop my own taste and I was constantly sharpening my eye. I began as a temp at the WB and left as vice president of talent and casting seven and a half years later. It was a supreme education. As tough as Susan could be, I knew I was being taught by an expert at the top of her field, and I developed, by pure osmosis, the ability to identify a breakout star. I remain forever grateful to her. I wondered what it felt like to be so powerful. She never appeared to be under pressure. I was so young, and in my view, she operated with complete resolve and knowingness. Her word was supreme and never challenged.

But nothing remains static, and I was soon exposed to my first corporate merger when the WB merged with the UPN Network to form the newly christened CW Network, staffed with 98 percent UPN employees. The WB team was unceremoniously dismantled and huddled together in the rain under one unemployment umbrella.

A few months post-merger, needing to work, I accepted an offer to cast a pilot as an independent casting director. I was thrilled and ready to put my knowledge to work. Then, that job led to another. If felt great to be back in the field, auditioning actors every day, setting up casting sessions, presenting ideas to the producers, then to the studio, and on to the network.

I really did miss being on a team and part of a work family, so I reached out to a hot up-and-coming casting company comprised of two young male casting directors and their staff. I had known them both in passing, but not well, so I invited them for a margarita in the Valley. After some chitchat, I asked if I could join their company and turn the couple into a throuple. After some tricky financial negotiations (they would retain 90 percent and I would be paid 10 percent from the overall fee paid by the studio), they agreed. I figured taking a pay cut would be worth it in the long run. It was either more money working on projects alone or a chance to work in a well-calibrated casting office with a fantastic team on higher-profile projects.

Throughout the day, we would pitch casting ideas to each other, debate talent, skill, depth. We were so cross-eyed by the end of the long days that we were prone to fits of laughter to the point where tears would stream down my face. They affectionately referred to me as their "camera lady" because I would run camera as the more performative of the two insisted on reading with, and sometimes outacting, the actors during auditions.

I learned while working with them about the nuts and bolts of running a successful casting company while working on multiple high-end projects. We worked with so many talented producers and writers, such as Michelle Nader, Jenni Konner, Sean Hayes, Ali Rushfield, and Abraham Higginbotham; as well as directors like Jason Bateman, Richard Shepard, and Paul Feig. I was newly engaged to Max and creatively charged but financially challenged. My net income that year was sixteen thousand.

While working in our casting trifecta, Max and I got married. Twice actually. The first time we snuck away and went to city hall and told no one. After five years together (minus our four-month hiccup), we wanted one day just for us. We continued with our regular wedding planning, telling no one, and stood in front of our family and friends on the big day, smiling to each other as a married husband and wife of four months. Our ceremony was a perfect mix of Catholic tradition that also honored Max's Jewish heritage. It was beautiful and simple, and both families felt represented and celebrated.

A year later I received a phone call at our casting office from the head of casting for a major network/studio for whom our casting trio had just cast a pilot. She asked if I wanted to go to lunch and if I might be interested in hearing about a new position she was looking to fill. As happy as I was working with the boys, I was financially intrigued.

We met that week at Factor's Deli for what I would call an executive audition. She brought her number two, a cheerful and smiling co-pilot. He was Sonny to her Cher. She had been in the casting business for years. Her legacy began at *Sesame Street*, where she cast a very young Natasha Lyonne. She was chic, stylish, with a cropped haircut and an all-black wardrobe—think a fifty-year-old Faye Dunaway, cheekbones and all. She ordered a salad—no dressing, with dry crackers on the side—and told me that the position available would be a step down from my previous corporate title of vice president at the WB Network. I would be at a director level, with Sonny as my direct boss. "I have my eye on retiring at some point," she added casually, "so who knows, anything is possible." Honestly, I could not tell if she was being serious.

I smiled and listened, not commenting, already convinced that the step back in title would not be an issue for me. As we left, I had no clue if she liked me, if this lunch had gone well, or if I would be getting a call back. While in the valet line, she said, "I'll call you tonight," with no indication of what that conversation would be about. "Okay, thank you," I said graciously. I was excited.

Later that night she did call me. She was chatty on the phone, and told me more about the position, the salary, the benefits package, the stock. It was a very enticing deal—a contract position for three years, with a 401(k)—that was music to my ears.

Max and I were happy, broke newlyweds. The balance in his checking account was $325. There was no question we needed this. As much as I loved working with the boys, getting this job offer was the light at the end of a penniless, dark tunnel. At that time, Max was going out on auditions and hustling. He had picked up a guest star appearance here and there, but we had burned through all my savings from the WB Network. Though honestly, it didn't matter—Max was sober, we were more than content, and we were both doing what we loved.

Max was about one job away from landing something big. I would often say to him, in response to his impatience, "You are 'almost the guy' only so many times before you *are* THE guy." I had seen it from the other side: an actor getting so close to landing his breakthrough role, over and over. Max had tested against the same three guys—Bryan Greenberg, Adam Pally, and Franz Kranz—for the lead role in several different television pilots, not quite edging out his competitors. He was frustrated, which I completely understood. For actors, it's a test of your tenacity. You have to be relentless, remain hopeful, and eventually, if you're lucky, it will click.

"Faye" wanted me to meet with the president of the network. The next day, I tried shimmying into three different pairs of pants, unable to zip all three. WTF? Baffled by my expanding waistline, I threw on a jacket to cover an untucked shirt over unbuttoned pants and hightailed it to the meeting. Faye walked me (and unbeknownst to me at the time, a little fertilized egg in my belly that would grow to become Lilly) to his door and teed me up with an introduction. As I walked into his office, he swung around in his big leather chair, stood, and thrust his hand out.

He was tall, with country-club style, WASPish, but with that John Slattery *Mad Men* charm. He had a great voice and warm presence, a ten on the charisma scale.

"Slattery" was considered a TV hitmaker and talent whisperer. He had executive poise with affable energy and had also won respect and adoration from the creative community. It was usually one or the other. Suits who make tough decisions about creative art don't usually engender much trust from artists. He was the exception. However, female leaders were emerging and seemed to innately master talent relations at the highest level, fostering trust among the über-talented with apparent ease.

The meeting was casual and relaxed. Slattery asked me a few questions. He had been there only a year, having been brought in to manufacture hits. He had most recently been at NBC and had made his mark by developing and championing *The Office* and *Parks and Recreation*, both comedies in a new single-camera format stolen from the Brits' mock-you style with straight-to-camera testimonials. No more live audiences. This new form of comedy would be shot on film, in a studio or on location, mini movies every week. And from that one meeting came the job offer, which I excitedly accepted despite the step down to director of casting.

Wickedly funny and dark, Faye was fascinating to work for. She was so talented, I thought she was psychic on occasion—her casting track record was unparalleled. She had never married and, instead, had a long-distance French lover, an artist who was silver-haired and sexy—think a salt-and-pepper Vincent Cassel. Many executives, casting directors, and agents found Faye elusive and aloof. She was private and somewhat mysterious. I found her to be straightforward and a total badass. She was so nice to me, and never expressed anything but support and respect.

Faye loved and appreciated actors, the way only another artist can. And talent loved her right back. She was a pro, completely uninterested in office politics, and above trying to impress people. She was there for the art of it and would often duck out of parties and events, finding them superfluous.

One afternoon shortly after I started, she popped by my cubicle and said, "Come on. I want to introduce you to Kathryn."

"Oh, okay," I said, jumping to my feet, not knowing who she was going to introduce me to. We walked across the lot to a dressing room trailer outside a huge soundstage. Faye knocked on the door. "Hello?"

A female voice shouted from behind the door, "Coming."

The door opened and Kathryn Hahn appeared, slightly disheveled and buttoning up her shirt, while tripping over something . . . and in the most lovable KH way, she threw her arms around Faye. She was there shooting a pilot that Faye had cast her in. Faye had signed Kathryn to a talent holding deal, which meant she was exclusively to work on our TV pilots. Their immediate familiar rapport told me that these two had history. Faye was like a cool aunt and Kathryn was stepping into the spotlight she provided. I was so enamored by how Faye as a *suit* related to Kathryn as an *artist*. I remember thinking, *I want to build that kind of ease around talent*. Kathryn's warm presence and accessibility oozed star quality. I just felt it. And I still do whenever I see her.

A year and a half into the job, Faye approached me as I was perched outside her office. "You've been identified," she said. "People have noticed. I told you when I hired you that I was working on my exit strategy, and you are it."

It was not a question or a proposal. Much like when Susan decided I would stay at the WB, Faye had decided I would be her successor and that was that. I was shocked. Yes, she had told me that she was planning her retirement when she hired me, but I had only worked for her for eighteen months. And I had been on maternity leave for a month and a half, having my firstborn, Lilly. At that time, I felt like I had a straw in my mouth, feeding me oxygen from one day to the next.

"Yes, I remember you said that, but I need to think about it." She ignored my hesitation and proceeded with the plan to pass the baton. Faye knew her exit was contingent on finding a replacement; she was a woman on a mission and unwilling to entertain my self-doubt. It wasn't necessarily about me; she wanted out and I was her ticket.

I wanted to cry out: "I'm a new mom; I'm not ready for this," but the moment I would start trying to talk her out of it, Faye would shut down my protests. She had cast me in the role of her successor with the same conviction that she would cast an unknown actor she had seen do an Off-Broadway play. Her sentiment being: *I've seen all I need to see. You are built for a bigger stage.* Faye had done her time in corporate America and was counting down the days until she could move back to New York City and live the life of a now-much-wealthier bohemian artist.

Slattery, the network president, met with me many times over the next several weeks and months and was so enthused by Faye's endorsement that he also would not consider a plan B. He approached his negotiation with me like this: "Tell me what you need to feel good about saying yes." There was no getting out of this. Faye's exit date of September 2011 was on the books; it was happening.

The person I talked to about what kind of support would help me succeed in this role with such a huge jump in responsibilities was my dad. I had him on speed dial. "Hi, it's me. In my contract, they are offering a four-year term. Should I ask for a shorter amount of time? What if I'm not happy?"

He calmly responded, "No one is going to keep you in a job you don't want to be in. I looked over the agreement you sent, and technically, it's four years with an option at year two. Think about achievable milestones at the midpoint. Ask how they measure success."

"Okay. Thanks, Dad. I'll keep you posted."

Two hours later: "Hi, it's me, have a sec? They have asked

me to write formal reviews for the staff. I don't feel comfortable doing that yet."

"That is a very reasonable request for a department head. Tell them you would like more time to adequately evaluate their performances. Also, ask if they would hire a corporate coach to help ease your transition to management."

My ascension continued and I was eventually promoted to executive vice president. I worked there for eleven years. Along with the bright team of executives I hired, we launched talent scouting efforts internationally and promoted showcases in comedy, where our mantra was "people who make us laugh." In this time, pre-Netflix comedy specials, we featured newcomer Jerrod Carmichael, a nineteen-year-old Pete Davidson, Ali Wong, and Ronny Chieng, with the night often hosted by talent from our on-air shows, like Lil Rel Howery and Michelle Buteau. We would invite comedy executives, writers, and studio executives to the Improv Comedy Club, where we held showcases featuring the talent that we'd handpicked. Now I was the boss lady on the other end of the line when my executives called in from festivals to report on their talent scouting efforts.

I built my own work family, I traveled to sets where we shot shows, and I courted talent, unknown and known. My life felt big. With each passing day of experience, my casting instincts grew, as did my evolving management style. It was a dream job that I loved as much at the entry director level as I did at the EVP level. Every day felt different, and there was a constant influx of new people joining the growing company.

I was inspired by the new challenges that were presented.

I took great joy in mentoring staff and other young execs. Just as Faye and Slattery had believed in me and accelerated the trajectory of my career, I also felt a need to pay it forward. I, too, would take a leap with someone who I knew had it in them, maybe before they knew it themselves. Everyone needs someone along their career path to recognize and champion their potential. I have been lucky enough to be on the receiving end of that and I have also been that person for many actors, and I stood up equally as strong in support of my colleagues.

In February 2020, I had a girls' dinner with my two besties, Joyce (think Reese Witherspoon) and Shannon (think Linda Cardellini), at our favorite neighborhood restaurant. I raised my glass and gave a toast: "To the best days of our lives. We are living them now!" Each of us was on a career high, our parents were healthy, and our husbands and children thriving. I felt so lucky and knew what a unique moment in time this was. All the hard and focused work of the last two decades on our respective career paths had resulted in robust success. Joyce had developed and launched her own television series on ABC. And Shannon had just been promoted to president of marketing at a major studio, overseeing half a dozen divisions. We were all feeling very grateful.

Cue: John Mellencamp's "Crumblin' Down"

4

Broken Picker:
And Why I DM'd Britney Spears

I am and have always been a Britney Spears fan. I wasn't down at the courthouse with a "Free Britney" sign, but I had participated in conversations about her conservatorship and certainly sided with the movement for her to reclaim her autonomy.

A few years back, I flew to Vegas to see her Piece of Me show toward the end of her residency at Planet Hollywood. Had I known then that she was basically a prisoner on her own stage, out of respect I wouldn't have danced and sang along so enthusiastically. I do know the lyrics to most of her songs. I bought the *People* magazine that had pictures of her wedding with K-Fed. I am not bragging, but I have stored in my long-term memory her sons' names, Sean Preston and Jayden James—information absorbed by living in Los Angeles in the early aughts. I have, however, not had the pleasure of meeting Ms. Spears myself (yet).

I was genuinely happy when she met and married Sam Asghari, and concerned when they announced their divorce.

About a week after the Sam/Brit breakup announcement, I was flipping through Instagram and landed on one of her dance montages in a bikini top and cutoff shorts. The next story was about how she was getting away on a vacation. I thought, *Yes! Turn down the noise on all the divorce drama and media speculation. Good call, Brit.*

This revelation got me thinking. *Who is she going away with? Is that rumor about the affair with her bodyguard true? And where the F are her girlfriends? Where's her tribe of gals from back in the day? Who is her support system and why isn't said group directing her to the right stylist for better hair extensions?* How hard it must be for her to make friends, to trust people. She has 42 million followers, but how many friends?

The casting director in me took over: I needed to cast a new best girlfriend—and eventually a new boyfriend—for Brit. I had honed my ability to "pick the good ones." So I took to my Instagram and sent her a Direct Message. It read as follows:

> Girl, I have been following you forever. You need a solid girlfriend, a friend who does not want or need anything from you. Someone who has your back, with no ulterior motives. I am a mom, and a sister, and have a husband and my own full life. There are normal, good people who live in Los Angeles. You don't need to settle. Anyway, I am thinking about you and hoping that you have a bestie who can support you through your divorce. We are rooting for you. If you ever want to hang or need advice, we got you. Xo, Tess

Okay fine, the offer to "hang" at the end took it a bit too far, but I genuinely meant it. I can't stand to see her struggle and I really am rooting for her. I want Britney to be surrounded by good people who care about her, and I am not sorry for putting an invitation out into the ether to help. Obvi, she never wrote back, but I stand by it. And maybe someday she will accept the offer, and we will hang in my kitchen on a Friday night with cocktails and a cheese plate with my funny, kind friends with no expectation of anything in return.

When I told Max I had DM'd Britney, he just looked at me and said, "Hold on a minute." Then he took out his phone and hit record, wanting to document this moment. "Okay, so what did you do?"

"I DM'd Britney, offering her some support while she's going through her divorce with Sam. And I also invited her over if she wanted to hang."

Max laughed and laughed and said, "Of course you did." He wasn't the least bit surprised. This kind of thing is very on brand for me.

It is not unlike the time we were at a small party over Oscar weekend 2021 and Taylor Swift was standing two feet from us. I said to Max, "Oh, there's Taylor. You know her, she did an episode of *New Girl* season two." (Note: She *did* do an episode of *New Girl* in 2012, but Max didn't have a single scene with her.) Max's eyes widened as he said, "Tess, do nooooot—" Too late. I had already leaned over and said, "Hey Taylor. Hi Joe." (She was still dating Joe Alwyn.) "How are you guys? You know Max." I looked at Max. He was horrified and frozen but was forced to engage as Taylor threw her arms open to give him a hug. The four of us stood talking for about twenty minutes, laughing like old friends.

I would have DM'd Taylor when she broke up with Joe, but she was on tour and has always been surrounded by a solid girl squad to get her through any heartbreak, so I didn't feel the need to reach out. As far as girl squads go, I have always envied these groups of eight to ten girlfriends who met in high school or college and remained close. They are the bridesmaids at the weddings, the baby shower throwers, the tribe that takes group vacations. They share the lifelong intimacy that comes from knowing people through various stages of life.

That just did not manifest in my own life. We moved so much as kids that, aside from my one bestie from middle school, Ryan, my older sister, Christina (think Melanie Lynskey), is the closest to a lifetime mirror that I have had. Christina is the yin to my yang. We are so different that we complement each other. She is an intellectual introvert . . . which I guess by comparison makes me a shallow extrovert? She is traditionally smart and glided through college and law school. She is earnest and focused. I have always looked up to her and been amazed by her clarity and conviction. I feel fluffy next to her. She is the badass attorney, breadwinner, and PTA mom. She will lobby and challenge norms for the betterment of the whole.

My memories of us from childhood are those of me, younger sister, following behind her, looking out for her. She kept a steely forward focus, paying little attention to the aftermath left in her wake. She always took on the biggest challenges and dove in headfirst. When we relocated to Texas, she signed up for the talent show at our new school to sing a solo of Journey's "Don't Stop Believin'" while playing air guitar. In grade school, I used to chase her out of the house as she strapped her typewriter, flute, and enormous book bag to her bike, with hastily arranged pigtails, yelling with two bobby pins in my hands, "Don't forget to pin your wisps!"

I had a perfect view from behind her to make different decisions based on the consequences she experienced. I was her observer and could navigate my own choices with much lower stakes. Christina pushed the boundaries of teenage rebellion with my parents. By the time she left for college, she'd paved a smooth road ahead for me: They were worn out, and I was a bit wiser when it came to breaking the rules.

She was labeled "bold," whereas I was described as "cautious." She was considered "classically beautiful," and I was described as "cute." I have more ethnic features—bigger, rounder, and darker in every sense—nose, eyes, butt, boobs, hips. She leads with the left brain, more practical, and I lead with the right brain, more creative. She always put herself out there. I felt plagued by introspection in comparison. I moved slowly through decisions, where Christina would declare her next move with little thought, and usually succeeded. On any given day, she would proclaim things like, "I'm going to be the first female quarterback in the NFL. I'll be in the backyard throwing the football if you need me."

I admired her confidence and breadth of knowledge. I felt like an outsider within our traditionally intellectual family, as Christina engaged in heated debates with my parents around the dinner table on any number of subjects, while I sat quietly daydreaming. It's ironic that now as a parent, I have a sensitive, cautious listener in my son, Ozzie, and a passionate *jump now, worry later* joiner in Lilly. What a test of my patience when Ozzie wants to know every detail about a situation before agreeing to participate. *Hi, boy-me.*

My process of examining pros and cons slowed me down socially and later in dating. By contrast, my sister married one year out of law school and divorced a year and a half later, then married her ex's polar opposite and divorced again eight years after that. To this day, I see her ability to take the leap and bet on herself as her best quality—she is all in or all out. I live more on the fringe, identifying potential, making strategic, thoughtful decisions, at times to my own detriment.

As an adult, despite Christina's proclaimed happiness and comfort with being single—and I believed her, because she had a successful career and two fantastic kids, and was living her best independent life—still, I couldn't help it, sometimes I questioned her degree of fulfillment. I believe we are built for companionship. The comfort that comes from knowing someone so well, you know what they are thinking without their saying a word. Doesn't everyone want to be deeply understood and unconditionally loved?

I am flawed and clearly annoying, but Max loves me and my idiosyncrasies. If he finds me lovable at my worst, I can't be that bad, right? I longed for Christina to experience that same thing. She deserved to have a bad day and be adored anyway. As does Britney.

That was one of the reasons why, in 2019, when a close colleague said to me, "Your sister sounds great. It's her picker that's broken," I was prompted to take action. *Ding!* I am a good picker; I do it professionally. Without her knowledge, I decided to build a profile for her on a dating website. I wanted to try my hand at casting her a boyfriend or, at the very least, a sexy fling.

Max and I got together pre–online dating, so I had never created a profile and was determined to build a masterpiece. I needed real-time intel on what was really working on the scene. Luckily, I worked with a bevy of single hotties of varying ages who happily educated me on the dos and don'ts of the apps. And I had plenty of pictures of my sister from family events and from her Facebook page.

I know what you're thinking. *Mind your business, Tess. Did Christina express any sentiment about being lonely?* No, not exactly. No, she did not. But I can't help myself! My soul would not rest until I knew I had done my part to maximize every ounce of potential. (Ya hear me, Britney?) Yes, that was the price of admission of being my friend. Sorry. What can I say? I care!

And so it began. I crafted a beautiful profile with pictures, listed hobbies, her ideal geographic dating area, her kids, her trips, and her pets. My single sources said that sporting event pictures always fared well, so I put up pictures of her at the World Cup decked out in USA gear, along with pictures of her hiking with her dogs and surfing. Under the career portion, I added a short, vague blurb with lawyer jargon. After two days of tweaks, boom, boom, click, and uploads, we were *live*.

I felt proud of how authentic and honest her profile looked. No crazy doctored photos, just a non-bloated narrative about Christina and her life. I know it sounds like a stretch to use the word "honest" when she had no knowledge of this profile's existence. So what that she had nothing to do with it! It was all TRUE.

Besides, I am a matchmaker by profession. A writer paints a picture of the character on the page, and I try to find someone who can embody all those characteristics. This particular situation just happened to involve casting the role of a potential love interest for my sister, because, like Brit, her picker was broken.

Once I had the gorgeous profile up and running, I let Max in on the plan. "Babe, check this out. I made a dating profile for Christina. I'm going to screen a few candidates for her."

Max, confused, said, "What are you talking about?"

"I built a profile for Christina—well, technically, I guess you could say I built a profile *as* Christina. But I'm just getting the ball rolling until I can set up a face-to-face meeting for her. I mean, you must agree she could use some . . . 'support' in meeting a nice guy."

"Wait, so she is down with this plan?" he asked.

"She knows nothing about this. It's a surprise. My gift to her."

Max stared at me for a beat before saying, "Umm, this is called catfishing, and I think it's illegal. And even if it isn't technically illegal, it should be—you CANNOT do this, Tess. You are committing fraud." He continued ranting, but his voice faded away as my thoughts drifted to Christina sitting across from a handsome gentleman at a candlelit dinner, beaming as she gazed lovingly into his successful, single, age-appropriate eyes.

A few minutes later I came back to the moment, and Max was still talking, listing all the reasons why this was a bad idea. I looked up at him and smiled. "It's okay. You don't get it. It's a sister thing."

Not only did he not get it, but he was also vehemently opposed to this entire plan. Yet I would wake up every morning, take my laptop to the kitchen, and read aloud to Max about Christina's prospective suitors, despite his objections. "Stop. Please stop reading this to me. I don't want to be a part of this or be complicit in any way. And you also sound ridiculous."

"I do not. I'm really good at small talk! I'm great at getting my casual flirt on. Listen to this: *'Hey, Tom from Oakland. I am doing well, trying to figure how someone with such an impressive job also has time to stay in such great shape. You must live in the gym.'*"

"Oh God." Max rolled his eyes.

"Are you questioning whether or not I still got game?"

"Nobody says 'got game' anymore, so yeah, I am questioning it. What does Tom from Oakland even look like?" Max asked.

I turned my computer for him to look at Tom's pics. Max surveyed them for a minute. "I mean, he is in okay shape, not incredible . . . 'living in the gym' is a stretch."

"I don't disagree. Obviously, you are in way better shape." Max smiled. "But you would be shocked at how far basic flattery can get you." *Gotcha, Maxie.*

My plan all along was to come clean with Christina after I

had vetted the candidates and scrutinized the tedious details of each interested suitor. It was something she did not have the time or patience for, whereas it was second nature to me. I have a gift. I am an expert at reading through the bullshit, professionally and personally. This was just me using my gift for good.

Every morning I would sit at the kitchen table and weed through the too old, too young, too dumb, straight-up creepy, and reply or not reply appropriately. And sure enough, I/Christina began a conversation with a wonderful man named Nelson, a single dad with two kids similar in age to hers. He lived close to me/her in San Francisco and had not done any online dating before. Perfect. We talked back and forth every day, getting to know the details of each other's lives. My mornings were spent giggling at our witty exchanges, while Max stared at me with disdain and disapproval.

On other days, Max would sense an impatient tone or slight attitude from me and ask, "What's up?" I would say, "Oh, nothing. I haven't heard from Nelson today." His response: "Oh my God, this isn't real. What are you *doing*?!" I became slightly indignant that no one in my life agreed with this loving and clever plot to scout for lovers for my sister. I didn't see it as catfishing, *per se*. I was cupiding.

One night while having dinner with our neighbors and dear pals, both writers, one of whom had just published a book on morality and ethics, our friend surprised me with his outrage on the subject: "You have been lying to this nice, innocent man by pretending to be your sister?"

"Yes, but I haven't been lying *about* her. Everything I wrote about her is 100 percent accurate and from the heart." Judgy stares all around. "You really think this is wrong?" I asked.

"YES!" he said. "Without question. This is deceitful. You are lying to someone. In fact, I feel uncomfortable even hearing about this."

Max basically leaped up from the table to take a victory lap. "See! I told you, Tess. I have been telling her this from the beginning. Now you have a published author on morality telling you."

Geez, chill, bruh—we're talking about a dating app, not Kant's moral imperative. But truthfully, I didn't feel like I was misleading Nelson; I was being truthful AS Christina. What's not to get? I know her strengths better than anyone. I was just infusing her already wonderful qualities with a little extra confidence, just turning up the color a bit.

After about six weeks of talking/writing almost every day, I asked Nelson if he wanted to meet for coffee. We had come to know each other well enough; it was time to explore the in-person chemistry. In the meantime, I had done some stealth recon and discovered that Nelson was an ER doctor at a hospital near my sister. As we continued to correspond, I began to get nervous. God forbid, Christina happened to roll into the emergency room one night with a bout of strep throat. Nelson would be like, "Christina, hi, it's me. I can't believe we're meeting face-to-face like this." Pause. Longer pause. "It's Nelson."

And she would be like, "I'm sorry, you must have me mistaken for someone else," sounding like an amnesiac Drew Barrymore at the end of *50 First Dates*, as Nelson/Adam Sandler proceeds to recite everything he knows about her in a bid to win her affection, except Christina would find it creepy rather than charming. We had to get a date on the books. I was eager to take this budding relationship live.

However, much to my disappointment, after dozens and dozens of flirty exchanges, Nelson said he needed "more time" before meeting in person. I found this pace mysterious and his lack of urgency to meet me/her intriguing, but I persevered. I had to keep this going until he felt ready.

I appreciated that Nelson wanted to take the time to build a solid foundation with me/Christina before we all fell for each other. It showed a seriousness of intention that I found reassuring. I fantasized about our families vacationing together.

Then on a cold November morning, I received a message from Nelson. He wrote that he really liked me but that he had met someone else on the site and they were dating exclusively, so he didn't feel right about continuing to communicate with me. *Wait. What?* I know, I was floored, too. He said he wanted to be (GOD, DON'T SAY IT!) "friends." *FRIENDS???? You have no idea who you're talking to, buddy.* (In fairness, he literally had no idea who he was talking to.) *I'm a professional picker! I pick for a living! Don't make me regret picking you!*

Not gonna lie, I took the news pretty hard. Max was hardly sympathetic.

"Are you seriously upset that Nelson dumped you? I can't believe I just said that. Do you see how abnormal this all is?!"

I nodded in acquiescence, then lamented, "But Nelson broke up with me/her before I/Christina had my/her shot at a face-to-face date. I don't get it. What did I/she do wrong? Why didn't he pick me/her?"

Max couldn't resist the jab. "I guess your GAME isn't that strong." *Ouch*. Fair point.

I wrote a strongly worded message back, then deleted it. Wrote another one, deleted it. I ultimately decided to take the high road, with a *less is more* response. "I am happy for you. Good luck. Christina."

For Christina's birthday later that November, we agreed to take a girls' trip to Palm Springs, just the two of us. It would be the perfect time for me to finally break the news about the catfishing. Hopefully she would be so relaxed she wouldn't get upset. We would meet for three days and two nights, indulging in spa treatments, having late lunches followed by afternoons poolside with a bottle of rosé. I was excited to get out of my daily grind.

We shared a room and gave ourselves permission to order room service and eat in bed. Only Christina can appreciate the charge that comes from breaking a long-instituted Sanchez family rule: *Eating in bed?? In your pajamas?? Nooo!!* I could just imagine my mom fainting from mortification.

After our first night, while eating a sumptuous breakfast in bed, it felt like the right time to break the news.

"Chrissy, I have something I need to tell you."

Sensing my more serious tone, she got up and sat at the edge of my bed. "Okay," she said expectantly.

"I really want you to be happy and find love again," I said. "But you haven't been dating, and you're not even trying to meet someone."

She said quietly, "Uh-huh."

"Well, I decided I would screen some candidates for you."

"WHAT?"

I whipped out my laptop and opened it up to show her the profile I had made.

"Oh my God. Where . . . how did you get that picture? And that one?" *I had her on the line.* "Oh, he's cute, a step in the right direction," she said. *Hooked.*

"Well, actually, this is not a step, this profile is live and has been for about three and a half months. I've been corresponding, *as you*, with a few men, one in particular. His name is Nelson."

And then there was a very long pause, as in no words spoken.

"Here." I handed her my computer. "Go ahead. Take a look at me as you."

I couldn't read her expression. Was she mad? I looked in her eyes and saw skepticism—a familiar look I often get from Max that says: *What did you do now?* She clearly needed time and space to process. She picked up my laptop and retreated to the café table on the patio off our room. I glanced outside periodically to try to judge her reaction as she surveyed Nelson's profile, reading several months' worth of our exchanges, holding my breath in suspense as she combed through her/my history with him.

After nearly an hour, Christina came back inside. She sat

next to me and put her hand on mine. "Thank you. Thank you, Tess. No one has ever done anything that thoughtful for me before." I looked at her, flooded with relief. "And also, eff Nelson! His loss! *We* played that perfectly."

Postscript: Christina took over my/her dating profile for a while but is currently dating a southern dreamboat from Texas who we knew growing up. My friend Britney, however . . .

5

Pablo:
Star of the Feature

It was a Friday in August 2020, six months since the March pandemic lockdown, and we were gearing up for more remote work, more Zoom school, and more isolation, when my phone rang.

"Hi Mom. What's up? How are you?"

In a quiet voice she replied, "I'm at the post office, mailing you something."

"Why?" I asked. "We're in a pandemic. What's so important that you would need to go to the post office?"

After a long pause she continued, sounding so weak, with no power in her voice. "I got your dad's CT scan back."

"What did the doctor say?"

"That's what I'm mailing to you."

"You're mailing me a report of Dad's brain scan? What does it say?"

She whispered, her voice crackling. "I can't say . . . the word."

"What word?" I asked. "So, it's bad news?"

"Yes," she said. "I can't say the word out loud," and she began to weep.

For months we suspected something had been wrong. My dad had lost a lot of weight, and he had been slipping further away mentally since the pandemic began, with no social life and limited external stimulation. Now, my mom held two manila envelopes with his fate sealed inside, one for me and one for my sister. Her only way to cope with the contents of that report was to have us read it for ourselves. But there was no way I could wait two days, wondering and worrying.

I took a deep breath and asked, "Is it Alzheimer's?"

Long pause. "Yes."

Longer pause. "It's very advanced." Followed by more weeping.

A million things raced through my head, but I felt the need to reassure her. "Everything is going to be okay, Mom."

My heart broke for her in that moment; she must have felt so scared and so alone, digesting this diagnosis. The pandemic was a lonely time for everyone, but finding out this news about the love of her life and partner for more than fifty years was taking an off-ramp headed in a different direction.

About five months earlier, Dad had been diagnosed with aphasia—the clinical definition being damage to the frontal lobe that affects the language center of the brain linked to speech. While he would know what words he wanted to communicate, he couldn't access them. We were still reeling from the decline in his ability to speak. My dad had been a wordsmith, a calm voice of reason, constantly doling out sage advice that we all counted on—everything was manageable, solvable with just a phone call or a conversation. Through his words, you could always be assured it was going to be okay. Always. Now we faced this unforeseen additional diagnosis of advanced Alzheimer's.

During every transitional time in my life, my dad provided me wise counsel. He was self-made, the first person in his family to graduate high school, college, and graduate school, studying psychology and earning an MBA in communications. He paid for his own education at Loyola Marymount University and Boston University with grants he received after joining the air force. He was neither ashamed nor proud of his humble beginnings.

My dad was devoted to his parents and always showed them deep gratitude and love. Mis abuelos were kind, simple, quiet, and so very proud of both their sons. I have such fond memories of seeing them during my childhood. As parents, they were strict and raised dutiful and respectful Catholic sons. My dad and his brother were held to high academic standards and achievement. As a result, from a young age he remained focused on building a life of abundance, with education, and a solid spiritual foundation.

As a result of that upbringing, my dad was not much of a playful or silly father. He never shared stories around the dinner table about crazy, high school antics. He never went out with his buddies, probably because he didn't have a group of buddies. He also would never use the word "buddy"—his were friends and acquaintances.

Every morning of my entire young life, before jetting off to work, he would eat breakfast in a suit and tie, with his distinctive aftershave and perfectly combed black hair. His casual weekend look was always a crisp, starched, button-down shirt and khaki pants. That is about as relaxed as I would ever see him. I never, to this day, have seen my dad in sweatpants or a non-collared shirt. He presented warm but pristine.

My dad was a master at public speaking and mediation. He could merge opposing sides of an issue with a calm, thoughtful resolution. His job as a business consultant at various firms was to help two companies, post-acquisition, come together and assimilate into one combined corporate culture, down to advising which corporate policies from each company should remain. Sometimes that included layoffs that he himself would be tasked with handling or that he would coach internal management on how to carry out humanely.

For example, if McDonald's bought Burger King, my dad would be called in to observe both cultures, speak to management on both sides, and spend from six months to a year coming up with the best vision for the new company—maybe calling it McDonald's King—by combining values, goals, even economic projections. It took someone like my dad, who could see above the fray, to distill the best parts of each company and form one unified mega-conglomerate inside and out. He had to travel internationally and spend time at company headquarters all over Asia and the Middle East. He traveled so much that my sister and I used to joke that he was in the CIA. He wasn't, I swear. CIA, if you are listening, we were joking.

My mom said when they met, she was immediately drawn to his kindness and ambition—as she put it, "Both qualities age well over time." The subtext being: An attractive, nice guy who lacks drive was not a good choice, and a very successful, driven asshole who was not nice also would not do. I know both my parents agree that Max is undeniably kind and considerably more playful, while also being hardworking.

My dad was a meticulous rule follower—by the book, no shortcuts. He would hold us accountable for both our good and bad decisions. His parenting style was rather strict by today's standards, loaded with the same high expectations he was raised with. On weekends, there was no sleeping in. Every Saturday, even when we had friends sleep over, we were woken up to do our chores. Nothing about our house or upbringing had a chill vibe. Time was never wasted.

Every Sunday morning, rain or shine, we attended the nine a.m. church service. Did I sit through some services hungover during my high school years? Sure did. Attendance was non-negotiable. My sister, Christina, had a strict midnight curfew. If she was two minutes late, she would be grounded. I watched all this from the younger sibling seat and was appropriately terrified of breaking the rules.

At sixteen, Christina was given our abuela's old Ford Fairmont to drive us to and from school. This car was the actual make and model of a police car: a square, white, four-door sedan. It was so old that the FM radio only worked when you slammed the ashtray that was located below the radio—yes, you read that right, an actual ashtray in the car. This beauty had camel-colored seats with manual crank windows and no air-conditioning. The front seat was a bench, so no matter who sat in the passenger seat, the bench would stay at the appropriate distance to the steering wheel and pedals to accommodate my sister, who stood at five feet two inches. This car became legendary in our high school parking lot. "Here come the Sanchez sisters in their cop car."

Once, when Christina was about seventeen, she had lied about where she was spending the night. My parents happened to be out early in the morning running errands and spotted the white beauty parked at a strange location. My dad pulled over, got out so my mom could take the wheel, and he drove the Fairmont back to our house, with my mom following in the car behind.

A couple of hours later, my sister called in tears to tell our dad that her car had been stolen. He asked whether it had been stolen in front of Karen's house, which was where she was sup-posed to be. Christina had to admit the location of the theft, and out came the confession of where she had spent the night. My dad never yelled in this sort of situation, or any other. He simply told her they would discuss it when she got home. Sometimes I wish he had yelled. That would have been better than the calm conversation he would have with us expressing his disappoint-ment, which made us feel far worse than him yelling ever could.

Upon her arrival home, Christine saw her white Ford Fair-mont parked in the driveway, not stolen. Our dad greeted her outside and told her he had driven the car home, and she was grounded for lying. Point for Dad.

When I was sixteen and Christina had left for college, I inherited that same Ford Fairmont. The things that car has seen.

One evening in early May, I drove my bestie Ryan and two other girls to a party down in Mission Beach, which was about twenty minutes from our house. The two girls in the back seat were sharing a bottle of Budweiser. I made an illegal U-turn and was pulled over by the cops, who promptly found the beer and issued me not one but *three* tickets: one for my traffic violation, one for being underage and in possession of alcohol, and another for driving with an open container.

Three tickets?! I was beside myself and knew I was maybe not going to be allowed to drive ever again. Yet being sixteen, we of course still had to go to the party.

The next day I studied the summons and tried to strategize how to approach this situation with my parents. The court date was set for August 31, nearly four months away. So, I made the logical teenage decision to put a pin in the conversation and not ruin my first summer of driving. May turned into June, June into July, July to August, until . . . wait for it . . . the evening of August 30.

I heard my dad closing up the house before bed and said, "Dad, can I talk to you for a minute?"

"Yes, of course."

"I really screwed up; I am so afraid to tell you," I said.

"Go on." Ever so calm.

"Well, one night about four months ago, I had two girls in my back seat, and they were drinking a beer, and I got pulled over for doing an illegal U-turn. They found the beer, and now I'm afraid I might be going to jail. I'm so scared." The anxiety over this pent-up secret from the past four months came rushing out in tears. "Are they going to take my license away? I didn't even know these girls."

"When is your court date? And may I see the tickets?"

"It's tomorrow." Crying more.

"Okay, I don't know what the court will say, but I do not think you will be going to jail. I won't let that happen. Be dressed and ready to leave by seven thirty."

The next day, dressed in a suit and tie with briefcase in hand, he took me to court. I stood next to him as he addressed the judge. He was so cool and collected. He handled the whole incident as if I was his client, with poise and confidence. He negotiated for me to have it erased from my driving record, with a fine, traffic school, and an all-day class about underage drinking and alcohol education. He never raised his voice or even grounded me. I paid the fines out of my savings from my summer job. The two days of classes were my penance.

If you met my dad, you would always be greeted with warmth, kindness, and incredible politeness. So polite, he would ask before he gave advice, "May I offer you some insight?" then gently guide you to reflect and think. He stood to welcome every person who entered the room, offering something to drink or eat and a place to sit. He remembered everyone's name and what made them special. He noticed the details and would often inquire after those details. If you were cold, he would offer you a shawl. If you sneezed, he would offer you a pristine handkerchief from his pocket. He was so thoughtful, never missed a birthday or an anniversary.

My dad readily offered advice, and as I got older, he became a consultant in my love life. He often referred to my ex-boyfriends as wreckage I left on the side of the road. One of my boyfriends in high school continued to stay in touch with him even after we broke up. My dad had to console him: "May I offer some observations? It seems to me Tess wants to be on her own and have a true college experience. I understand that this hurts." I finally had to tell him, "Dad, they don't get to continue to be your friend if I am not dating them anymore. Please cut communication."

He was so proud of my perseverance and the life that Max and I had built together. As a grandfather, he adored being with Lilly and Ozzie. He used to play the piano with Lilly, and she would sing, exactly how I did when I was a child. As with many grandparents, he was more playful with them than he was with us growing up, his role of Dad was one of duty.

Although my career choice may not have been immediately understood, I achieved success through the same level of hard work and focus without a road map, just like him. I am a product of my father's work ethic. He loved to talk about the corporate goings-on at my work. It grew into a driving purpose in our relationship, and I was happy to have such a strong point of connection.

Now, as I write this, my dad's eyes still know me, and his smile is filled with joy when he sees me, but he cannot form words or sentences. He is silent. He needs help to dress, to get in and out of bed, and to shower. This once-dignified man has an aide seven days a week helping him with his basic needs. He can't comb his hair, play the piano, or read music, he can't type or write. His powerful presence and commanding force have deteriorated into a childlike existence, absent of any authority over his own life, with my mom watching this daily decline in real time, each day a centimeter further away from their once-tight clutch of beautifully entwined lives.

Witnessing my dad slowly crawl toward the end was unbearable. On one visit, he stood up from the couch, went into the hall closet, grabbed his old briefcase, and as he was heading out the door, in garbled words said, "They are waiting." I couldn't help thinking his angels were waiting for him—his parents, whom he adored. I wanted to assure him that we would be okay, that he could go whenever he wanted to, and yet the thought of releasing him felt impossible.

I've thought about all the conversations we've had, about the pride he felt as he watched me grow my career and go from leaving a wreckage of exes to being in a happy marriage with two healthy children. He had worked so hard his entire life and given us so much. My happiness was his success. But our dynamic had shifted. I was no longer in the familiar role of daughter seeking his advice; I became his parent, directing him and making decisions on his behalf—we all did, especially my mom. We had to step up and project the same calm and strength he had always shown us. I wasn't ready for this role reversal, especially not with him. I wanted to opt out, though that was not an option.

My mom treaded in the waters of denial. It's unimaginable what she was going through. But, always cheerful, she continued a routine of three meals a day, seated with linen napkins, place mats, and proper place settings. For all meals, walks, and outings to Costco or speech therapy, my dad was fully dressed in a collared shirt, V-neck sweater, and khaki pants with laced shoes. He would sit in the backyard garden while my mom filled the silence with happy anecdotes of our past. Sometimes I would get a text that said: "Just talking with dad about the time we drove cross-country to visit Alice and it poured rain the whole time, but we still had a great time." I think that happens when the present is too painful; reliving the good memories keeps us going.

For me, any feelings of joy felt muted, with a portion of my heart reserved for him, a sectioned-off place, in quiet protest. *He can't feel joy, so this area of my heart remains inaccessible, in solidarity with him.* My heart was on lockdown. *Sorry, Joy, this seat is reserved for Pablo.*

6

Tío:
One of One

"**B**angsgiving?" I said into the phone. "No way, that is hilarious! Please send me a pic."

My BFF, Chazz—think a John Mulaney type—had called to tell me that he was in West Hollywood and had spotted a promotional poster wrapped around a bunch of streetlights, advertising a "Big Gay Party," complete with a shirtless photo of Max and cartoon turkeys on both shoulders like angel wings, with "Bangsgiving" splashed across the bottom.

My phone dinged. I looked at the poster and started laughing. OMG, *it's perfect*. I ran to find Max.

"Babe, Chazz was just in West Hollywood and saw this poster everywhere." I handed him my phone.

"This is a work of art!" he said, laughing hysterically.

"Did you know about this?" I asked.

"No, but that looks like it's going to be one hell of party. I am honored to be the poster boy." He sent the picture to himself.

"And I am honored that my man is the face of gay parties in West Hollywood. This is the kind of fame I can get behind."

It was the Sunday before Thanksgiving, and both of our phones began to ding throughout the day, as different friends began texting us shots of the poster from various spots in WeHo. That evening, Max posted the picture to Instagram, wishing everyone a "Happy Bangsgiving," and has done so every year since 2019. (That phrase was actually the title of a Thanksgiving episode of *New Girl*, in which Max happens to be shirtless, embracing a frozen turkey.) In fact, Max was so flattered, he showed the flyer on the big screen of *The Ellen* Degeneres *Show* when he had an appearance later that fall.

Max was a familiar face in the West Hollywood scene, thanks to me. When he and I started dating and we assimilated into each other's lives, I couldn't wait to introduce him to my chosen family. I traveled in a tight gay posse, and I tossed Max smack in the middle of it on Kilkea Drive with my quirky troupe of players. We came as a package deal.

It was a Friday evening in March 2003, within the first month of our budding romance. We pulled up to the house of my closest bestie from my WB days, aka Vince Vaughn. We entered to find Halsted (think William Jackson Harper, a television writer) and Dan (think Drew Tarver, an up-and-comer in talent management). They had been together about a year.

"Hi guys, this is Max." They smiled and said friendly hellos. Behind us was a bunch of other pals whom Vince had introduced me to. We plunked down around the dining room table. It was sink-or-swim time for Max, as they sized him up and down.

We ordered dinner, cracked open a bottle of wine, and fell into our familiar banter, which usually included some gentle ribbing. Tonight on the storytelling block, Halsted was telling us about an audition tape he'd just sent in for a new show called *Queer Eye for the Straight Guy*. He had Dan film him as he spoke about why he was the perfect candidate to speak about culture. Apparently, it took a few takes to get it right, and we sat on the edge of our seats, hearing about each swing. Everyone weighed in on what they thought should have been on the tape, but alas, it was too late; the tape had already been submitted.

Vince was not sold on the concept of the show and expressed his doubts: "Are you sure you can't get that tape back?"

A flash of doubt crossed Halsted's face. "Nope, it is too late."

Max chimed in with his support of Halsted and melded into the group seamlessly, so at ease in every setting. I slipped into the kitchen to get another bottle of wine, and Halsted followed and said, "Max is great . . . and this is a tough crowd."

"Right!" I said, thrilled by his immediate endorsement. I was so relieved there was no Sophie's Choice to be made between my besties and the guy I was beginning to fall for. The feelings of admiration were mutual, and new friendships were about to take shape.

The most fun I ever had, the hardest I ever laughed, the hardest I ever cried, has always been in the warm arms of both this chosen family and my biological one. There's a certain intimacy that comes with the territory, a shorthand and an innate understanding. I feel an immediate mutual acceptance and recognition with gay men that defies categorization. Maybe because I know what it feels like to be an outsider. I was always the new kid in every class trying to fit in, constantly feeling like I didn't belong.

Gay men have always been my safe space. It was not until I went to college and met peers who had not grown up around a gay community that I realized this was not the norm. For many, their education on gay culture came exclusively from the ground-breaking show *Will & Grace*—and thank God it did. For me, the shiny bright light I had always known was my first gay idol, icon, and best friend, my tío Ron.

I was born in Germany and spent my early years there, so I didn't meet my uncle Ron and his now-husband, who I lovingly referred to as Aunt Thomas, until I was about five. I had heard about my extended family on both sides but had yet to encounter any of my aunts and uncles. After my dad left the air force and we returned to the United States and relocated to Wisconsin, he announced, "My younger brother, Ron, your *tío*, he and his boyfriend are flying in from California to meet you and your sister." My dad adored his younger brother—even at five, I could see and feel it. There are eight years between them, and their roles were firmly in place: that of an older, wiser brother and a fun, younger brother.

From an early age, my dad felt a duty to look out for Ron and protect him. I witnessed this amazing mutual understanding and love from both men, and when Ron and Tom showed up in chic denim ensembles and coifed hair, I was instantly enchanted. Photos of the occasion show us sitting on our front steps, with me beaming at this beautiful person. It was like, "Guys, I found him! The playful, more extravagant, freer version of my dad!"

I look like Ron, and I laugh like him. He is a big, joyful force who will wink at you across the table with a robust laugh that fills the room. We both love to sing; he was blessed with a beautiful voice . . . me, not so much. I inherited his sense of fun and his sense of humor and the ability to flirt with both men and women, as well as a love of fine hotels and excellent customer service.

I adored our time together. Ron and Tom took me out for lunches, shopping excursions, and sleepovers. It's no wonder I instantly migrated toward all my gay colleagues in the workplace— from John to Vince and so many other top decision-makers in entertainment whom I befriended along the way.

I met Ron and Tom's friends and colleagues, and our families celebrated holidays together. They always design elaborate tablescapes for every holiday, which often take an entire day to stage. And I love a dramatic reveal—I'll bring a covered cake stand to the table just to be able to rip off the lid and present a perfectly accessorized dessert with artistically placed berries. Hello, family genetics. I call it "creating a moment." Ron taught me how to make the mundane feel special. All you need is a little creativity and extra love to put into the details.

Ron and Tom have a charming custom of naming each home they have lived in, usually after one of their dogs and ending in Run, Manor, Hacienda, Chateau, or Villa. They treat their dogs like people. They are photographed for their Christmas card in tasteful holiday outfits every year. And they have oil paintings of each dog they have raised hung around their house in thick, ornate gold frames, like fine art in the Guggenheim.

Ron is a successful interior designer and, ever since I can remember, has owned his own design firm. Tom is an artist, a painter, and an incredible chef. They met in the mid-seventies at

Mother Lode, an iconic gay bar in West Hollywood. As the story goes, it was love at first sight, and the connection between the two, undeniable. They quickly cut ties with other prospective suitors and were exclusively a couple after one week.

Shortly after moving in together, Ron brought Tom to meet my *abuelos*. Their acceptance did not come easily or immediately. It was almost a decade before Ron and Tom would be truly welcomed as a couple around my grandma's table. My grandpa, ever so sweet and kind, came around a little sooner.

When Tom came out to his family, they rejected him completely. He never returned home, and they never met Ron. Their huge loss. Ron and Tom were together through the AIDS crisis, and they grieved many of their peers and friends who passed away. They endured challenging homophobic times and tolerated less-than-kind behavior from people, but their love has only grown and remains stronger than ever. Their life today is picturesque in a cozy home in Maine filled with their dogs, a wonderful community, and us, their family.

My dad and my uncle both found Midwestern blondes who adored them. The only wrinkle in this blanket of warmth has been the occasional icy exchange between my mom and Tom. Maybe it's *because* they have so much in common, both being artists who love their Sanchez men. But any tension between them has never affected the wonderful bond my dad and uncle share. They would just chuckle as the cats marked their territory with passive-aggressive suggestions hurled back and forth.

One Thanksgiving, while I was in high school, we hosted Ron and Tom at our house in San Diego. My sister and I thought we would add to the celebration and get stoned before we sat down to eat, so we snuck outside for a quick toke. The tension between the competing spouses was running so high that everyone was completely oblivious to how high *we* were. And we were baaaaked.

We sat down and my dad thoughtfully said grace, as he always did. With an "amen" and a busy flurry of dishes passed around the table, *let the games begin*. Mama Sanchez with the serve, a slight jab lobbed into Tom's court. His return: an Olympic-level double eye roll back at my mom. She volleyed a swift return. We were spectators at a grand slam match with the two of them going back and forth, as they sipped their red wine.

"Do you follow a recipe for these mashed potatoes? These are a bit dry. I tend to prefer a creamier constitution."

"Well, pardon me, I didn't realize Julia Child would be grading this meal," and then under her breath, "a-hole."

WAIT, did I just hear my mom say that out loud?

Tom plucked his napkin from his lap and tossed it on the table as he stood. Things were escalating very quickly, but also in slow motion due to my stoned haze. Tom marched into the kitchen, grabbed the pie he had brought, and stomped out the front door.

What. Just. Happened?

In under a minute, my mom was on her feet running after him to apologize, as we trailed behind. When we got outside, we couldn't find him anywhere, despite repeatedly calling out his name. Next thing you know, Ron was backing the car out of the driveway slowly and idling in front of the house. Like a genie, Tom popped out of the thick ficus hedges with his arms tightly wrapped around his boysenberry pie, and he slipped into the passenger seat as if escaping hot lava. My mom was beside herself as we watched their taillights speed away into the night.

During this epic showdown, my dad and Ron remained totally calm and, dare I say, slightly amused by the *Succession*-level theatrics. Bewildered, Christina and I quickly retreated to our bathroom to recap this battle royale. As we sat on the floor, whispering out of respect to my mom, who was stewing in the other room, our concern evaporated into fits of uncontrollable laughter. We were both laughing and crying at the same time, too stoned to string words together. It was a mess, and honestly, the most dramatic turn of events we had ever witnessed in our family. This was not a fighting household. A DEFCON 1–level dispute sounded like, "We are very disappointed in you."

The next day, heartfelt apologies between the Sanchez spouses were exchanged. They each claimed to have had one too many pre-dinner cocktails, and thankfully, peace was restored. My mom and Tom have both mellowed as they've gotten older, and there is an increasingly relaxed rapport between them now. Tom will call me and make a point of saying what a great talk he had with my mom, and she now proudly claims ownership of their tight bond.

Cue: Christina Aguilera's "Ain't No Other Man"

Ron visits me every time he comes to Los Angeles for a client meeting. During a trip in 2004, I invited him to dinner at the apartment I was sharing with Max. I had told Ron about Max, and they were eager to meet. I set the stage with music, candles, and a heaping bowl of pasta, and in walked my *tío*, bringing with him a gust of love and energy. We gave him a tour of our place and settled in for a night of getting-to-know-yous. Ron and I immediately slipped into our shorthand, and he and Max totally hit it off. The evening was perfect.

As Ron stood to leave, he opened his arms to Max and gave him a farewell hug: "Now, honey, you take good care of my Tess."

Max assured him he would, and smiled as he closed the door, then turned to me and said, "You and your uncle are the same person. I totally get it now." Welcome to the family, Maxie!

When Max and I were married in 2008, California had just passed the law allowing gay couples to marry. Ron and Tom flew in from their home in upstate New York (called Mol Run, after their dog Molly). While they were in town, they made an appointment at the Los Angeles County Registrar and got hitched just a day before our ceremony. They attended my wedding as a fully realized, legally recognized, married couple, and I was eager to acknowledge this long-awaited official status.

When it was time for me and Max to give our toast, after thanking our parents and friends, I spoke about how honored I was to share our night and celebration with Ron and Tom, the other newlyweds of the evening. I was so proud to bear witness to their union, a love that had waited decades to be recognized as equal in the eyes of the law. I invited them to join us for a toast to true, everlasting love, and then to join us on the dance floor. Max and I shared our first dance as husband and wife, and

Ron and Tom shared theirs as husband and husband, the four of us dancing side by side.

I caught Ron's teary eyes over Max's shoulder. His face beamed with pride as he mouthed, *Thank you. I love you.* I mouthed back, *Me too.* It felt like my whole relationship with Ron had been leading to that exact moment. Holding space for them was both a small and a big thing—small in that it was so natural and easy to do, and big because it was historically significant. This was not lost on anyone, and there was not a dry eye in the place. My dad looked on so proudly as he watched his beloved family in one joyous celebration.

Many years later, in 2020, that wonderful day seemed so far away during the loneliness of the pandemic. Ron and Tom were sealed away in their Maine residence that they'd lovingly named Mabel's Manor. We Zoomed on all the major holidays, but it was painful as we watched my dad become more and more vacant, with fewer and fewer words. We were all enduring this sad and disconnected experience, seeing it together, but unsure if we should acknowledge it or simply ignore it with idle chatter.

As a child, I remember hearing my dad on the phone with Ron every Sunday. They would talk about all sorts of things, and what really struck me was how relaxed and happy my dad always sounded while speaking with him. That is one of Ron's gifts, his unabashed benevolent spirit. I recognize now that the unconditional love and respect was not exclusively for my dad, but for every person lucky enough to be in Ron's life. But, as my dad was beginning to fade, so were their clearly defined roles.

The conversations between Ron and me were also changing

as we both struggled to adapt to this feeble version of my dad. We spoke honestly, and our talks often circled around to our own mortality and what we both hoped for and wanted for ourselves as well as Max and Tom. I felt how hard it was for my uncle to step into his new role—the younger brother caring for the older brother who'd always looked out for him—but he handled it with such grace and compassion. For me, experiencing this tragedy of losing someone while they are still alive was shocking. With every new step downward into what felt like my dad's abyss, I called on Ron for support.

One afternoon I sat in my car after a recent visit with my dad, telling Ron about the full-time nurses who had taken over his care. I wept as I acknowledged how much Dad would hate this, having strangers showering him and grooming him, as he has always had so much dignity and composure. Through his own tears, Ron assured me Dad no longer had the ability to feel things like embarrassment or shame. This provided me so much comfort, especially coming from Ron, who so deeply understood the before and after. He knew the fortitude and strength my dad moved through the world with. That wonderful strength was as reliable as the perfectly pressed, folded handkerchief he had tucked into his suit pocket since the beginning of time.

It's so painful to watch someone's physical and mental vibrancy, once a booming shout, become a whisper. My heart also broke, knowing my uncle was losing his best friend. It was a rare dynamic in their generation for a gay man to come out to an older brother and immediately receive a lifetime of unwavering support, especially coming from a Catholic Latino family. Ever the protector from day one, my dad opened his arms and heart to his younger brother. Their brotherly bond only became tighter over time.

What a gift to have these two very different yet defining paternal figures in my life. I would not be who I am today without my *tío*'s wonderful influence. And I'm so grateful that both Lilly and Ozzie have come to know Ron and Tom. They are the lucky beneficiaries of growing up around examples of loving companionship of every kind.

Cue: David Guetta featuring Kelly Rowland's
"When Love Takes Over"

7

Click to Join This Zoom:
Series Cancellation

The day was like every other during the pandemic. I sauntered through the kitchen, laptop in hand, to our work room: small, cozy, and wallpapered, with a big wooden desk, velvet-upholstered chairs, and a flat-screen TV on the wall. It was a great space that was now being used for high-stakes video conferences, craftwork, gift wrapping, a secret hideaway when Max wanted to play Xbox, and the perfect location for filming Instagram videos during quarantine. (Thank you, Lilly and Max, so Insta-famous.)

It was late August 2020, the height of the pandemic, and everyone was home. My state of mind was fair: quarantine sucked, COVID-19 vaccinations were still a long way off, and my dad's Alzheimer's diagnosis was about a week old.

The kids had finished their Zoom school for the day, and Max was preparing their dinner. I had a 5:30 p.m. Zoom meeting with my boss to discuss upcoming bonuses for my team and me. My boss was the president of a major television studio/network/streamer. Think Joseph Gordon-Levitt—he has that same twinkle in his eye, dark hair with a sprinkling of Clooney-esque gray creeping in around his temples.

"Joe" and I had been working together in different capacities for years and we were fantastic together. There were times we would be in a meeting and without saying a word to each other, just with one look, we knew exactly what the other was thinking. We shared similar creative tastes and a sense of urgency to make the content and cast of each show great.

Before COVID, around 6:30 p.m. on Fridays we would gather in his office to recap the *bests* of the week. We would all be a bit punch-drunk from the long hours, and his assistant would often have to close the door as the laughter got a bit raucous. Joe had a great sense of humor, which is rare for somebody who had ascended to his level. Often, as you rise in the ranks in these pressure cooker entertainment executive positions, it's easy to lose sight of the fun and irony of situations. But not Joe; his giggles were fully intact. In fact, Max and I had just made a heartwarming and funny video (requested by Joe's wife) as a surprise for his fiftieth birthday.

So, there I was on Zoom, making small talk with Joe for ten or fifteen minutes before he got down to business. As Joe transitioned to the bonus discussion, what followed was a flood of compliments about my work over the last quarter: my keen eye, my attitude, my fantastic team members, praise for reaching the targets I was tasked with hitting, and my consistent strides forward despite the pandemic, concluding with a significant bonus number for my efforts.

"Well, thank you," I said, pleasantly surprised. This, after all, was during a time when the fiscal health of the entertainment industry had started to wane, production had slowed, and new protocols were being implemented. I was feeling incredibly fortunate, and the bonus exceeded my expectations. I was then told the bonuses to be distributed to my teams in Los Angeles and New York, which were also generous.

As I expressed my deep gratitude and general love of my role within the company and working for him, I noticed Joe starting to squirm in his seat. Something seemed off. He appeared to be uncomfortable in accepting my words of gratitude. Then, breaking eye contact, he mumbled, "This is very bittersweet."

"Bittersweet?" I said. "Why is it bittersweet?" I assumed he meant because we weren't speaking in person, as in days of old. I felt it too. I couldn't wait to be back in the office, face-to-face with everyone. But the look on Joe's face was a different expression, one I hadn't seen before. It was a look of pain. Something was very wrong here. *What was bittersweet?*

Before my mind could catch up, my body began to react. I felt my pulse racing. The air became thick. My breathing intensified. And my eyes were locked on Joe's face over a Zoom background of the Leaning Tower of Pisa. (Oh, the irony.)

"This is bittersweet because we have decided not to renew your contract." He pushed the words out painfully, as if he were passing a kidney stone. Stunned silence was followed by what I like to call: *Crazy lady getting kicked off* The Bachelor.

"WHAT THE FUCK? Is this a joke? Are you fucking serious? I have been here for eleven and a half years. I have hit every target, and—your words—I am really good at my job. I am diverse, over forty, and one of only a handful of female executive VPs in the company." I don't remember much of what he said after that. But I did manage to get out, "Who else is getting laid off?"

"No one else. Just you." He continued, "They have decided to take the department in a different direction, and they are eliminating the department head position, but in the interim, the role will be overseen by X. (X being the amazing person he had hired eight years earlier.)

It was clear that Joe was just the messenger. This was awful for him, too. I could see it in his eyes, written across his face, in his body language. He was like a doctor delivering a fatal prognosis to a patient previously believed to be in perfect health. I could tell this was not going the way he thought it might. He was scrambling to adapt the script human resources had given him.

When a contestant doesn't receive a rose on *The Bachelor* and is sent packing, they usually show footage of the woman storming out of the house. In shock after a long, emotional night of shooting, she is then asked to do a straight-to-camera testimonial. I bet some of the castoffs don't even remember what they said to the camera, but I guarantee it was in no way the best version of themselves. It always ends with a vacillation between tears, straight-up anger, and belligerence.

I am embarrassed to admit that I had the exact same reaction. I, too, was swinging between sobbing and white-hot rage. I was also in a complete state of shock. I stepped outside my body and looked down at myself, and all I could think of was the phrase I had so casually tossed out hundreds, maybe thousands of times in my career: *We're going in a different direction.* And this time, it was being said to me.

As my mind reeled, I tried to get ahold of myself. *RETAIN YOUR DIGNITY. RETAIN IT. Leave the Zoom before this goes on one second longer.*

Did I heed my own advice? NOPE.

Instead, I kept saying a phrase that I have never used before or since. I don't know why or where it came from, but this specific sentence was on repeat, both out loud and inside my head: "So, this is how my story ends." Then tears. Then right back to: "So, this is how my story ends." I was like an actor trying to find the rhythm of a line. *Let's try it again, Tess, but this time with more anger: THIS IS HOW MY STORY ENDS! Again, Tess—now try it sad and slow: This. Is. How. My. Story. Ends.* Followed by more sobbing.

From the kitchen, Max heard my voice getting louder and louder, and he came into the room and was completely thrown off by the catastrophic meltdown he'd just walked into. "What's happening? Why are you yelling?"

I responded in certified crazy-person voice: "I just got fucking fired," quickly followed by a certified crazy-person high-pitched laugh.

Max sat down in front of me, his whole being suffused with compassion. I knew that look. I was also still on camera, while Joe was doing his best to console me. He went rogue from his HR talking points: "Tess, I don't want to lose your friendship. I really care about you."

A series of jumbled thoughts ran through my mind: *You*

don't want to lose my friendship? You didn't stand up for me. You didn't advocate for me. You didn't give me a heads-up. You allowed this to happen. How can we be friends? Instead, what came out of my mouth was . . . yep! . . . "So, this is how my story ends," except this time I *sang* it. *Once more with feeling, Tess!* "THIS IS HOW MY STORY ENDS." *Now with anger and heartbreak!*

Max stood up and came around the desk, a lifeguard saving a drowning child from a violent riptide. He stepped into frame, face close to the camera, looked into Joe's eyes, and said, "THIS IS OVER." He slammed the laptop closed and took me in his arms for a hug that held up my entirely limp body.

I have recounted this story so many times, and it's still so vivid. My response was in no way the best version of my higher self. In fact, I can no longer watch *The Bachelor* and witness a once-confident woman humiliate herself—it's a serious trigger. Thank God Max ended the spectacle, because I could have stayed on that Zoom, sobbing and repeating that phrase for at least another three hours.

I can't minimize the reality of my feelings that day or my disproportionate response. It felt like the ultimate betrayal; I believe the term is "blindsided." I was invested in my job—some might say *overly* invested—but I was just as deeply invested in the bonded relationships I had built there. I had worked so hard to get where I was, and I take full responsibility for my lack of work-life boundaries, but my job fulfilled me in ways I can't overstate. If I'm being honest, much of my self-worth and identity came from that position I treasured so much.

The nonrenewal of my contract was not a reflection of my performance or the affection that my colleagues felt for me. I remain close friends with so many of them despite no longer being involved in their daily lives. Eliminating my role was 100 percent a financial decision resulting from the economic strain of the pandemic. Five people got to keep their jobs in exchange for one person losing theirs, and that one person was me. But it all still really fucking hurt.

I had been tempted by job offers from other work suitors over the past year, but I chose to remain loyal. And now I'd been stripped of my voice, deprived of control over my own narrative. There is no question in my mind that the way the news was delivered was completely botched. If it was me having to lay off a colleague and friend whom I cared about and respected, I would not deliver the news on-screen. I would take a fucking COVID test and drive to that person's house and discuss it outside, like a real human being. Sorry. It's been nearly four years since that fateful Zoom call, and I'm still running hot.

So many hardworking people like me, and specifically women, lost their jobs in 2020 and 2021. I certainly was not alone, and unlike so many others, I was fortunate enough that my dismissal didn't jeopardize my living circumstances or hinder my ability to take care of my family.

I don't think anyone, least of all me, could have predicted just how unhinged I would become on that horrifying Zoom. It was wildly out of character. I am many things, but hysterical I am not. Yes, the job I loved deeply represented stability and provided much-needed structure to my life. I know my reaction would have been different had I not also been trying to metabolize the news about my father's prognosis, my feet more firmly planted on the ground. Had my dad's health not been declining, my first call would have been to him to strategize about my future. Now I was frozen. My whole life felt untethered.

I waited a week to call my parents to break the news. I needed time to prepare for a conversation that didn't start and end with me in tears. They were experiencing such drastic, sad changes in their own lives; their world was falling apart. I could not bear to give them the additional news of my unemployment to worry about.

I muscled up and started with, "The most unbelievable thing happened. . . . My contract is not being renewed." There was silence on the other end of the line, so I kept talking, trying to sound as upbeat and optimistic as possible. I continued, "It's not a big deal. This will be an opportunity for me to explore other creative endeavors."

My dad tried to cobble together some words. "Oh no, what happened?" More than his words, I heard the concern in his voice and felt it so deeply. As soon as I hung up the phone, I burst into tears. My job was my currency, with which we had always had such robust exchanges. Can you believe that as a grown woman—married with two kids—I felt ashamed to tell my parents? I didn't feel like such a grown-up anymore.

I wish I could say that my parents offered me unbridled belief and support, but that didn't happen. And that's okay. I had so much compassion for the life they were losing and their struggle to move forward. My dad's absence in this job reckoning was, and remains, incredibly difficult. All I wanted was to sit down with him and have a long conversation, to hear his wisdom. This was his area of expertise, his specialty. He had orchestrated thousands of layoffs and hundreds of corporate restructurings throughout his career and was masterful at navigating these situations with thoughtfulness and delicacy. How incensed he would have been by how carelessly it seemed to have been handled. But those words wouldn't come. Why is life's timing sometimes so cruel?

The question then was: *How to dust myself off and move forward?* I wanted a shortcut to minimize the pain and loneliness that hit me. Did I think it would be easy to get over the heartbreak and move on? *Yes!* Looking back now, I realize how many things had to happen before I could truly move beyond that major life shift. There was life before the axe-falling Zoom, and life after. I am still trying to figure out the after.

8

Striking the Set:
Painful Favor

The hours and days after that circus-like shit show of a Zoom are a bit of a blur. I rallied my people, all of whom I felt a deep attachment to, and informed them that my contract was up and that I would not be returning to the company. Keep in mind this was an hour after Max had slammed that laptop closed. I was still in shock. My main goal was to just keep it together and stay in control. I spoke each word slowly and deliberately, trying to get through it. Each of them sat there stunned and quiet.

I adored my team. I had hired them and had spent countless hours with all eight of them, more time in fact than with my own children. They were family. I had experienced their many life-defining moments, and they had experienced mine.

My journey at the company had begun when Max and I had only been married for fifteen months. Since then, I had given birth to Lilly and Ozzie and learned the fine art of multi-tasking as I figured out how to juggle work and children. I had witnessed my colleagues' marriages, divorces, births, and the passing of parents. We'd learned so much from each other and had all grown so much, both personally and professionally. I couldn't envision a way forward, or days spent without them—and without the work.

During the first six months of the pandemic, I had been in Zoom meetings or on phone calls for eight hours or more a day. And in the span of a single afternoon, I went from twenty years of having my foot on the gas to having my career come to a screeching halt. Total whiplash.

After all those years of feeling guilty for having to be somewhere other than with my family, now suddenly I was with them twenty-four seven in lockdown, with no colleagues to call and collaborate with, no team to lead, no talent to cast. It made me see Max, Lilly, and Ozzie through a completely different prism too. There had always been this other world pulling me away from them, a world that was entirely my own. Now it felt as though I was looking at three strangers. My sense of reality of our togetherness was askew without the barrier of my job. *These people in front of me surely couldn't inspire all my joy*, I thought, *certainly not by themselves, could they?* I was mourning the loss of the role of a lifetime, one that had filled me with purpose.

Though I put on a brave front for my team, the taste of my unfair dismissal remained in my mouth. My last phone call with Joe, the one just before the final Zoom, played on repeat in my brain during daylight hours and at night, when sleep wouldn't come. What had I missed? I had trusted this person. How could I have been so wrong?

As the news of my dismissal spread across town, I received supportive texts, phone calls, emails, and several handwritten notes from studio heads, past and present, television executives, writers, and dozens of actors, recounting how I had helped them along the way. One of the notes was accompanied by a notebook entitled *It's OK to Start Over*, with prompts printed on different pages, noting things like "Goals" and "Timeline." *So, all I have to do is fill in this little notebook, and I'll have all the answers I'm seeking?* Uh-huh, sure.

In those dark days that followed, the resounding message from my most trusted confidants, friends, and colleagues, even from people I didn't know very well was, "You are going to be fine, Tess." I heard variations of those words over and over like a tragic Greek chorus: "Other people would be taken down by this, but not you." All those years of trying to lead with tenacity had people believing I was resilient, even when I didn't feel that way on the inside. Still, everyone seemed to pick up on the narrative: *You got this.* One incredible former studio head and regular badass—think Lorraine Bracco—called me and said, "Honey, it will be a while before you get over this; take your time. Also? You're going to be fine." *But when?* WHEN?

Of course, there were a handful of people who didn't call. I see you and understand. I have been there, facing the need to make a call to someone who was experiencing loss or a total life shift. I would like to think that in my own life, I have made the uncomfortable call more times than not. I've learned from experience that there is such a thing as giving people too much space—it's always better to reach out, no matter how awkward it might be. With deep gratitude I remember the people who called to empathize or share advice or give me pep talks. Those conversations have stayed with me, and I play them in my head even now. I always left those calls feeling better and more connected, which was really what I needed most at that time.

Enter my former colleague and gay bestie, Chazz. Back then, he was the head of Drama Development, and his office was just two doors down from mine. Many of our conversations began with him asking me one question: "Does my hair look crazy today?" Nope, never. Honestly, he has the hair of JFK Jr. We became close almost immediately when he joined the company, and could often be found talking casting ideas and plot points on each other's couch during the day, along with regular office gossip. We had a symbiotic work relationship, always in creative lockstep, and our personal friendship blossomed over our ten years of working together.

As soon as I called him with the news, Chazz came over, opened his arms, and gave me the biggest, longest hug. (Yes, it was COVID, but we had to be together given the circumstances; he was my work husband, after all.) We drank wine and I rehashed all the feelings that were wrapped in the aftermath of the preceding few days. The comfort he brought me that night, not to mention all the other nights we have cried together over life's unexpected tragedies, is like no other. No one does a talk-through like Chazz.

"Tess, you need to know that I called the 'head boss' and

demanded answers and expressed my utter disbelief over this. I told him that I wasn't sure I could be at a company that does not support senior-level female executives. I also told him you had been a critical part of the success of the shows I have developed. I was so heated on the phone, I had to hang up. This is not okay. You deserve better."

"I feel so embarrassed," I said through tears. "Did you know that the COO had me lead a Zoom a fucking week ago with sixty executives about leadership and the creative process? I feel so humiliated."

"You are an incredible executive. I mean that. I am not just saying that because I'm your friend. I'm saying that because it's true. You have done nothing wrong. They should feel embarrassed about how they treated you. Tell me when you're ready to strategize next steps. I want to help."

"I need a few more days. I can barely think straight," I said.

A particularly dark movie reel that played out on repeat was the day Max came with me to pack up my office. It felt like I was packing up a huge part of myself, or at least one part that had pulsated with life-affirming vibrancy. We drove down a deserted street in a rickety U-Haul truck, silent tears streaming down my cheeks. With no radio to listen to or words to fit the moment, the atmosphere felt thick with despair. The eerily empty Los Angeles streets, normally so packed with traffic, were like a ghost town. Silence reigned within and without. My only condolence was that everyone was working remotely, so I didn't have to see anyone as I cleaned out my office. Thank you, Universe, for that tiny shred of dignity you gave me.

We entered the desolate building and walked into my office to find everything frozen in place since March 13: a cup of water, a notebook folded open to a page where I had written some numbers for an actor's deal, with the pen, cap off, perfectly placed next to the last word—untouched—exactly how I had left it seven months earlier. I had lovingly decorated my workspace with furniture and rugs. I had photos of our kids adorning my windowsill—a beautiful gallery from their births through toddler years and beyond—that I would regularly contemplate whenever I took a thinking pause. We packed up everything, including the nameplate on the door.

Another bitter pill to swallow was something I should have expected but hadn't prepared for. Less than three days after the Zoom, my work email was shut down, my cell phone was canceled, and my laptop was collected. Never having anticipated getting laid off quite so abruptly, I'd stored a lot of important personal information on those devices—the kids' doctors' phone numbers, school passwords, friends' addresses, personal and professional organizations. I no longer had access to that much-relied-upon information. I had been erased from my workplace. No forwarding email, just an automated bounce back: "This person" (not even my name) "is no longer here." It felt as though I'd been killed off with little explanation.

Months later, despite the loving support and guidance from all quarters, I was still stuck in my *Who am I without my job?* rut. I wasn't eating or sleeping. I needed this pain that was still so sharp, to dull. Enter Max, my sweet Maxie ICE (that is how I have him listed in my phone: "Maxie, In Case of Emergency"), who helped me trudge through the damage and repair. He is incredibly evolved when it comes to other people's issues. (Subtext: I said *other people's* problems. Even the most insightful people get blinded when they're standing nose to the glass.)

In the wake of my being let go, as the days became weeks and months, Max could feel my deep sadness. He suggested that as soon as *The Neighborhood*, a sitcom he was currently filming, wrapped for the season, we would spend a day together, just the two of us. No kid interruptions, no TV, no phones, a picnic at the beach perhaps, just me and Max in deep, fortifying conversation.

On the morning of our day-cation, I filled a backpack with lunch—sandwiches, apples, and popcorn—and loaded it into the car with two beach chairs and a picnic blanket. We drove west to Will Rogers Beach. It was a beautiful day in Cali, the cloudless, crisp blue sky bursting with sunlight. We set up our blanket and beach chairs and settled in with our books and mini portable speaker playing a mix of Francis and the Lights. Ahhhh, perfect. We talked about the future, my efforts toward moving on, what the summer might have in store, mostly revolving around what his schedule would look like.

Max said, "It feels like the world is finally resuming normalcy. I'm so excited."

Long pause.

"You're lucky," I replied. "I don't have a 'normal' to return to. Tomorrow is just another day. I don't belong anywhere."

"If you want to move through this, you need to forgive and get love back in your heart. Have you forgiven Joe?"

"Yes, I'd like to think I have."

"You know forgiveness is a two-person act. Write him an email. You don't have to send it. Think of it as a pathway toward some emotional elbow room and freedom."

Max's advice comes in two forms. The first type is rooted in the "Big Book," containing the guiding principles of Alcoholics Anonymous. Over the years he has been mentored by his sponsor and in turn sponsored others on their journey through sobriety. Most of the time, I find these evolved thought drops lovely, and also a tiny bit annoying. But not as annoying as the second kind of advice, which sounds slightly less evolved and is delivered in the form of a sports analogy. He will talk about a professional athlete I have never heard of, and with deep conviction, explain how my situation directly correlates to this player's plight. These bits of wisdom usually end with: "and consequently, the team really suffered for several seasons." Thankfully, today's advice derived from the wisdom he gleaned from AA.

"Hmm-mmm."

"Seriously," Max said, holding my gaze. "Thank him for the experience you had working with him. The root of your sadness is about the loss of the many wonderful things the role had provided. If you can become grateful, recognizing those gifts and experiences, that is where the real healing will begin. Write about what you loved, and give each memory a sense of place, like how much you enjoyed working with him on a particular project, or how great a certain table read was, or even just how much you enjoyed sitting in his office at the end of the week."

"Hmm." (Was this a pep talk or an assignment?)

"Just write it, please."

I stared into Max's eyes and heard the ease with which he rattled off this advice as if it were as simple as a math equation. *Yeah, just do this and this, and then this will happen. . . . See? Two plus two equals four.* My eyes welled and tears rolled down both cheeks.

Something happens to Max whenever I cry. His empathy seeps out and almost becomes a physical discomfort. *Quick, tie a tourniquet around this heart to stop the bleeding.* He's explained that it feels like a form of torture to him, and it demands action.

Max was unrelenting, so I said, "Okay." *Fuck, just shut up already.*

He told me he was going to go for a run and leave me in peace, and when he got back, he'd look at my email.

I confidently grabbed my phone and went to work on the letter. I started writing without a problem, listing some really great memories. I said that our collaboration was easy and creative and all you want in a boss-employee relationship. I thanked him for our time together. It actually felt good to write it out and spend time thinking about all those great times—there were so many.

When Max returned, he read the email.

"I love it," he said. "It's perfect. How do you feel?"

"Fine. Yes, sure, a little better."

"What's it going to take for you to send this email to him?

I really think you'll feel better. Doing this could set you free and untangle some of your congested feelings."

I listened and listened and listened, and Max kept talking and talking and talking.

"Send it. Send it. Send it." He stood up and grabbed a handful of seaweed that had washed up from the water, holding it with his arm stretched out. "You see this? This is your old position in the company and all the sadness around it. I'm stuffing this into my pocket. When you send the email, we will dig a hole in the sand and bury it. Your pain, sadness, and unrest will be cast out of your body, away from you, and remain buried on Will Rogers Beach, and that is where it will stay."

I picked up my phone, pasted the content into a new email, and hit send. Then I stood up, grabbing my own handful of seaweed and the empty tumbler we had brought with us. We ran down the beach and landed on the perfect place to start digging, using our cup to loosen the sand. Max took all the seaweed and placed it in the hole. He kissed me and asked me to say goodbye, goodbye to the resentments I was holding on to, and to the longing for my old life. I was desperate to be free from these sentiments that were holding me back. Using our bare hands, we furiously began to fill that hole with sand.

There was something ritualistic about feeling the grains of sand between my fingers and the tactile act of burying limp, soggy seaweed. And yes, I am aware that this sounds like a scene out of *Yellowjackets*, but I needed it. I had been carrying around the damp seaweed of despair like a cancerous tumor. These thoughts were poisoning me. The bitter farewell and the remaining uncertainty about my future was the last thought I would have before falling asleep each night, and the first thought when I woke up. I was plagued with this sadness wrapped tightly around my neck, and I was looking for something tangible to set me free. To breathe again without feeling that lump of despair in my throat, was the freedom I was seeking.

Later that night, I checked my email. I had received a beautiful response from my ex-boss. We eventually set a date to meet in person. When that day came, I felt ready to sit across from him, face-to-face. I arrived first and elected to be seated outside on the restaurant's rustic patio, with the sun just beginning to set. My promise to myself was to be honest and authentic. We had not spoken a word or seen each other for nine months since the Zoom. After the pleasantries about family, weather, blah blah blah, we got down to it.

He began, "I want to thank you for reaching out. I was so happy when I saw your email. I also want to apologize for how everything went down that day. I wish I had handled it differently. I've spent so much time replaying it in my head."

"I appreciate that. I wish I had handled it differently as well. I was really hurt. The shock of it combined with the recent news of my dad's health knocked the wind out of me."

"I am really sorry."

"Thank you for saying that."

We both acknowledged the "who" behind the marching orders and moved on from the heaviness, choosing not to delve into further details. We reminisced, and I was reminded why I had such fondness for him.

The encounter provided *some* closure. During those three hours, it felt good to reconnect, but I had no illusions that one conversation was going to be enough. I certainly didn't stand up and shake his shoulders and yell, "Why didn't you fight for me? How could you let this happen?" which is what I really wanted to do. And if I had, would his answers have satisfied me? Of course not.

In that moment, I thought back to one of my early talks with Chazz. He shared a story from his beautiful, late mother that really resonated with me. She was happily married until one day, her husband came home and announced he was in love with her best friend, and was leaving her. In one heartbreaking swoop, she had lost her husband and her closest friend. She was devastated, completely shattered, and couldn't imagine ever moving through and past the grief.

Despite her lack of hope, she soon met a man and fell deeply in love. From that point on, she referred to her ex-husband and ex–best friend's betrayal as a "painful favor." If she had not gone through that difficult time, she never would have met her new husband and had her two amazing children—Chazz and his sister, Louise.

Chazz said, "Look at the good that came out of my mother's pain. That is what this is. This is your painful favor, and I just know something incredible will grow out of this experience. You can't see it or feel it yet, but somewhere in this swamp of despair, there is a beautiful opportunity."

In the weeks that followed, I thought more about this re-framing. Could I eventually see this as a blessing? The pain stuck around for a very long time, and the favor is still taking shape. But just acknowledging that an experience can be both good and bad, both painful and hopeful, all at the same time, started to shift my perspective and prepare me for the other painful favors to come.

9

Head of Operations:
The H Suite

" **M** iss Mandy, I need to go to the bathroom."
"Christopher, please turn your camera back on. . . ."
"Excuse me, Miss Mandy? I need water."

"Katrina, we are not doing independent play. Can you come back to the computer?"

This is what pre-K Zoom homeschool sounds like, and it was every bit as hideous as it seems.

I no longer had my own Zoom meetings to escape to, and Max had been doing double duty with the kids for four months. So we decided to divide and conquer in the new school year, especially given my new unwanted freedom: I would cover Ozzie, and Max would continue with Lilly until his hiatus was over.

Anyone who has young children can probably now claim legit PTSD after helping their kids with mind-numbing Zoom-school distance-learning, five days a week. Teachers trying to give directions; kids going AWOL and logging off. An adorable pair of twins whose computers were set up in the same room created ear-curdling feedback every time either one of them tried to talk. The poor teachers . . . they were trying to teach letters and numbers while herding eighteen kitty cats. Even with me sitting there with him, Ozzie would occasionally be found lying under the table in protest, having shed various pieces of clothing. It was chaos.

I went from proposed production schedules, cast budgets, and actors' auditions to parceling out cotton balls, construction paper, and Popsicle sticks. AND I HATED IT.

Mostly, I stayed off camera. Sometimes I would lie next to Ozzie under the kitchen table, and together we would ignore Miss Mandy. I feel you, Oz.

In truth, I had not spent much time in an academic setting with my kids. I did morning drop-offs on my way to work and knew their basic strengths and weakness from parent-teacher conferences, but I was a working mom with the philosophy: *Call me if there's a problem, but I will assume all's fine unless I hear from you.* But boy, was I in for a rude awakening.

Like many people during that time, I was clearly depressed and, without my job, majorly understimulated. I craved challenges and adult conversations and was 100 percent sure that this type of life was not enough for me. I would fantasize about yanking the computer out of the wall and throwing it across the yard. The monotony was excruciating. I would also look at Ozzie and marvel at the fact that I couldn't recall ever having spent a six-hour stretch of one-on-one time with him. *Who is this kid?* I wondered. *How did he get here?*

I was full of self-doubt about my ability to mother him now that we were spending all this time together. Ozzie had come as a surprise to us at a time when both Max and I had established careers. We had not been trying, by which I mean we were *really* not trying, as in I-was-on-the-pill not trying. When I found out I was pregnant, I was shocked. Max, who was raised as an only child, was thrilled. In theory, we liked the idea of Lilly having a sibling, but we had not been actively pursuing the concept. With five and a half years between them, would they even share the same childhood?

When Lilly was born, Max did not have steady work, so he spent five months tending to her solo until she was old enough to attend the on-site day care at my office. He would pack her up in a stroller and walk to Starbucks to meet up with his two besties, Jerry Ferrara of *Entourage* fame, who was on hiatus from the show, and Kevin Christy, a stand-up comedian and regular at the Comedy Store. She hung with the boys, cooing as they talked fantasy football, acting, and writing. It was *Three Men and a Baby*, literally. Where many guys would crack after two days, let alone months of caring for an infant, Max was a pro. And I was able to get right back to work after six weeks' paid maternity leave, knowing Max, Jer, and Kev were looking after her.

Once Lilly started attending day care, I spent most days that first year popping in and nursing her during my lunch break. At the end of each day, I would pick her up, always getting there just before the seven p.m. closing time. Then we would make the trek home in evening traffic as I returned phone calls in the car.

When we pulled up, Max would greet us in the driveway of our rented duplex and unload Lilly, the diaper bag, my workbag, and my purse. Bags overflowing with bottles, scripts, DVDs, snacks (mine and hers), tissues for on-the-road spit-ups . . . he would take it all inside to unpack, and then, just twelve hours later, repack them all over again.

Lilly would spend her days at day care with nine other babies. They would talk to each other, babbling and gurgling and drooling. They learned to sit up, stand up, and eventually walk—one of the babies would start, and the others would follow, just like little ducklings in a line. When it was time for her to begin kindergarten at her new school, the transition was easy—no tears, just a confident wave over her shoulder. "Bye, Mom. Bye, Dad. I love you." I was barely away three months from that day care when I started to make the same drive across town with Ozzie, and the same wonderful teachers and caretakers who had tended to Lilly, now had a new Sanchez-Greenfield project.

I first realized I was pregnant with Ozzie on the teacup ride at Disneyland on Lilly's fifth birthday. A minute after the first spin, I asked Max for his baseball hat and promptly threw up in it. Lilly will never forget that visual from her first trip to Disneyland. I have a steel stomach, so I knew something was up. When we got home, Max bought four pregnancy tests of varying brands . . . all positive. But I was still skeptical.

I made a doctor's appointment, and within seconds of the ultrasound being placed on my stomach, there it was—a roaring heartbeat. "Wow! Congratulations," the doctor said. "This is a really strong heartbeat. From the looks of things, you're about nine weeks along." I remember crying, feeling overwhelmed by the reality of the situation. I didn't feel ready for another pregnancy while working or for caring for a newborn while working. Lilly was five and about to start kindergarten.

I called Max the second I got in the car. "Babe?"

"Hi, how did it go?"

I sobbed, "I'm nine weeks pregnant, and there's a really strong heartbeat." More sobbing.

"Why are you crying? This is great news! We can do this. We got this."

"We?" Sob, sob, sob. "The due date is in Aug-Aug-August." Sob, sob, sob. "Don't tell anyone. I need a minute."

Max tried his best to comfort me. "This was meant to be. This is going to make Lilly a better person."

"Okay," I said, but the tears just kept flowing.

My three-month ultrasound showed I was the landlady to a healthy baby boy who quickly wrapped his long, skinny body across my stomach and set up shop for what felt like forever. At that time, Max was shooting a role for *American Horror Story* that required him to bleach his hair blond and be twenty-five pounds lighter. I outweighed him by at least—I actually don't know because I stopped looking at the scale and told the nurses not to say the number out loud, but it was a lot. When it was finally time to have this squatting tenant evicted, his due date had passed, and I begged my doctor to induce my labor.

When the doctor finally agreed, we set the date and checked into the hospital at 8:30 a.m. I had been to all my appointments leading up to the birth solo, having come straight from work. I was not girlfriends with this doctor, but she seemed nice enough.

On the day of the induction, around 4:30 p.m. the doctor came in—picture Meredith Grey from *Grey's Anatomy*, season one Meredith, as I would soon find out, given her level of experience. She walked into the hospital room and said, "Are we having a baby today?" *We? Ewww.* No *we* are not, *I* am.

Max stood up, and I could see in her face that there was some recognition of who he was. *New Girl* was at its height of popularity in 2015. *Surely this won't become weird*, I thought. *This is goddamn childbirth.*

"Are you Dad? Hi Dad. I am Dr. Grey. Are you ready to have this baby?" *Dad?* Uch. Also, was *he* ready to have this baby? She was on my last nerve, and we hadn't even gotten started.

About twenty minutes later, she returned and announced, "Let's start pushing." She moved me into birthing position, legs spread, and instructed "Dad" to help situate me. After about fifteen minutes of pushing, Ozzie's heart rate began to slow. Well, this sent Dr. Grey into a frenzied panic. Not the tone you want during childbirth. Off came her watch, her jacket hastily thrown to the side, and two nurses entered and put a surgery smock on her. The nurses seemed to ignore her alarm and remained cool and calm.

"Okay, Tess, we have to get this baby out NOW. If it doesn't happen on the next push, we are prepping you for a C-section."

"What?" I said with mounting concern. "I thought everything was going fine. What is happening?"

She ignored my question. "Come, Dad, take her shoulder and shove it forward when I say go." As the nurse came around and positioned herself on my other shoulder, Dr. Grey screamed,

"On three! One, two, three—pushhhhhhhhh!" Nothing. "One more time . . ."

My body was getting thrown forward as if I was in a car accident. I glanced at Max, and he said calmly, "Look at me. Just look in my eyes. Everything is fine." I did as he said and completely forgot there was anyone else in the room as he held my gaze.

"Okay, good, very good, I got baby. Dad, come around to the end of the bed. Do you want to cut the cord?"

"No, I am going to stay right here. I'm good."

"Come on, Dad!" She was almost bullying him.

"No really, I don't want to." He was perfectly content by my shoulders, cheering from the stands with me, not down on the field.

"Okay," she said, and promptly cut the umbilical cord without clamping it first—the equivalent of cutting a running water hose, except this hose was filled with blood that splattered the ceiling and the walls with force.

After handing the baby to the nurse to be cleaned up and checked out, Dr. Grey sighed and said, "Wow, that was a close one." Then, without skipping a beat, she took off her bloody smock, put on her white coat, and said, "Max, can I get a selfie?" She already had her phone up and had moved next to him, while I lay three feet away, naked from the waist down, legs spread wide, feet still in stirrups, vag out on display, watching her take a picture with a blood-sprayed backdrop.

Can we all agree that was slightly inappropriate? At the time, we were so in love with and grateful for this healthy, beautiful boy that we barely gave it a thought. It wasn't until later, when Max and I recounted the events of that afternoon, that we started laughing hysterically at the absurdity. Later that month, I did get a handwritten note mailed to our home from the nurse who was with us that day from beginning to end. Turns out, she was interested in pursuing a career in acting and was wondering if I could offer her advice on next steps. Oh, Los Angeles, you never let us down.

Ozzie was sweet, chunky, and irresistible. His hunger was insatiable, and he devoured every drop of milk my body produced. He was round, with big cheeks, cherubic blond curly hair, and big brown eyes. His nickname was Cartoon Baby because he looked like a baby someone would draw if you were to describe a baby.

Now, five years later, in the middle of the pandemic, Ozzie was totally psyched to be home and thrilled to hang with his mom, who no longer had any distractions to pull her away. Eager to feel some kind of driving purpose in my life again, I decided to attack Zoom homeschooling with the same amount of laser focus as *Homeland*'s Carrie Mathison. *I know how to recognize potential and coax it out of a person at any age. I am going to coach Ozzie into mastering pre-K at the highest level. You work for me now, Ozzie, and the benefits package will include healthcare coverage and cookies.* Ozzie morphed into my new employee, and I was determined to lead him to excellence.

Did I do his assignments for him? Yes, I did—lots of coloring and letter tracing. Is he still academically behind as a second grader thanks to my ambitious appetite for his pre-K success? Yes, as a matter of fact, he is. (I blame COVID. Don't judge me.) If arts and crafts were on the agenda, by God, ours (his) were going to be the best. We made winter skiers out of cardboard toilet paper tubes, a menorah out of bananas and marshmallows, and stained glass out of tissue paper. School folders were color-coded; flash cards were written; systems were put into place. Even in PE class, which we did on Zoom with Ms. Louise, there would be no slacking on my watch. Drills were done in the kitchen and did not stop until we broke a sweat. We did relay races, jumping jacks, juggling, and hopping.

I was no longer hiding off camera; I was face-to-face with Miss Mandy, Ms. Dani, and Ms. Louise. We were in this together, day in and day out. I was a cheerleader, assistant teacher, snack waitress, organizer, and A+ enthusiast. Every once in a while, the teachers would give me a shout-out for participation in class, and I would actually feel a surge of pride. *I'm crushing pre-K, bitches!*

I was present with Ozzie like I hadn't been before, and really, truly available to my family for the first time in their lives. I wish I could say that being there felt better, more fulfilling, but it didn't. Instead, it felt like I was losing myself and just becoming an extension of my children. My role as a parent had always been about the broad strokes, not the minutiae of the day-to-day. It's probably horrible to admit that on some mornings I would think to myself, *Hey guys, don't get too attached to me; this is not forever, and as soon as possible, I'm getting the eff out of here.*

Meanwhile, Max was working with Lilly in the other room, making comedic Instagram videos about homeschooling that were inspired by his attempts to teach Lilly a fourth- and fifth-grade curriculum, and her disinterest in it. Frustrated parents from all over the country began reaching out to him, thanking him for the comedic relief. These videos struck a chord and were being viewed and shared by millions.

He was effortlessly winning both fourth grade and quarantine. His show *The Neighborhood* never got shut down. They finished shooting the final episode of the season the first week of March 2020. He worked on forty-four episodes over two years and did not get COVID. He wrote three children's books, inspired by his time homeschooling, shot several endorsements, participated in myriad charity Zooms, recordings, and PSAs; he did podcasts and talk shows. Max had never been busier. He was thriving.

We have never been competitive with each other, but this was a lot to digest. Everything he did or touched was a ten, whereas I was not even on the scoreboard. The only things I was consulting on were lunch, dinner, and a grocery list.

On the healing scale, I would say after a solid year without professional work, I was smack in the middle. Hollywood was in a hiring freeze since many productions had been shut down. Regardless, I was having meetings with execs across town. I was looking for a position at the EVP level, which rarely open up, and during the pandemic, people were not making any moves. I had been a boss, so I understood. Other bosses did not want to hire someone who recently had a position like the one they were occupying.

At one streamer, the casting head flat-out said, "Why would you want to work for me—on my team, mid-level—when you used to have my job?"

"I miss being on a team, and I am so passionate about casting, I would do it at any level."

While that was the truth, there is a delicate chemistry to any hierarchy, and they were not interested in what I was bringing to the table—namely, a lot of experience that would be *underneath* them.

I wonder sometimes if what I really missed about my job was the feeling of being important, that what I had to say, mattered. I had spent years refining my creative opinions and leadership skills, and now none of it mattered. I didn't have a voice that the people in charge of hiring wanted to hear.

I went to therapy for the first time in my life, read myriad self-help books, and listened to endless Oprah podcasts with the same questions always coming to mind: *What is my purpose? My raison d'être? What am I meant to do with my life now? What is holding me back from moving forward?* I had lost a community of like-minded people. I was once again an outsider kicked out of the club, the new kid looking for a place I could fit in.

I would take long walks to the Griffith Observatory, climbing the hills, often praying, calling out to the universe to tell me what to do. I would drive downtown to walk through the warehouses of the wholesale flower district. I felt anonymous and peaceful surrounded by plants and organized rows of fragrant, bundled flowers. I had a general malaise toward everything, with no projects to distract me. I know how ridiculously privileged and indulgent this sounds. But it's how I felt.

At the height of the pandemic, I'd gone through a manic period of pitching entrepreneurial businesses: I explored starting an organic cocktail company named Flaca; I considered launching a tablescape design company; I developed a few TV show ideas—anything to feel that productive spark. I had also redesigned and reimagined every bit of space in our house and completed home improvements. And I had crafted, taught, cooked, and worked out.

Yet I felt so alone on my journey, and I felt so guilty about feeling alone. I thought I was failing Lilly and Ozzie in my utter inability to bounce back. Needless to say, I was not at my best, for my family, or for myself.

Radiating light and always on the verge of the most thrilling reveal, Lilly is high-octane. Her hand is always raised, she is first in line, and she's at the center of every dance party. She was born that way. As a toddler, when we would be out at restaurants, she would flutter from table to table like a bird, smiling and saying hello. We soon adopted the name Lilly Bird for her, which later became Birdie, and now Max and I call her Bird.

She has a small frame with a raspy voice, and she often squeals with joy upon hearing . . . well, a lot of things. A sleepover with friends, avocado toast, news of a future trip, getting a new T-shirt, hearing her favorite song, anything related to Taylor Swift—too many to list. Even as Lilly becomes a tween, her demeanor remains the opposite of nonchalance, and that's her charm. As her mom, I know I'm biased, but at every phase of her life, I've been dazzled by her infectious spirit that grows bigger and more enveloping with every year.

In the early part of her life, while Max and I were climbing our respective career ladders, her understanding of normal was that her mom and dad had busy jobs, but when we weren't working, all our attention was poured directly into her. When I lost my job and my dad's health declined, I chose to allow her to see me broken. Up until that time, her perception of me was as an in-charge, problem-solving protector, as well as her number one fan. I was always multitasking, but I showed up for the important stuff to cheer her on. I remember leaving work a few times at lunch to help her class with holiday celebrations. She was so thrilled and proud to see me rolling up my sleeves with the other moms before I had to run back to the office.

She'd seen me at my peak, my happiest, fulfilled with my job, my family, my life. Then, all of a sudden, there I was, vulnerable and broken. I revealed an unfamiliar side of myself, the side that did not have all the answers. I wonder now what she will ultimately remember from that time. Lilly has faced academic challenges and struggles, so I felt it was important for her to know that she was not alone; even her tough mom struggled and cried. Here I was, heavy-hearted and empty, and I had shown my children that it was okay to be weak. But I also felt that was only valuable as a life lesson if I could balance it out with a demonstration of strength.

Some days Max would come home and say something like, "Oh, I see you reorganized the bookcase. That feels like a solid win for you." It became a running joke with the smallest of mundane accomplishments. Even scoring a good parking spot at Whole Foods, he was all, "Seems like a win for you." It went on for a while but eventually became more irritating than funny.

A few months into my new reality, I had the opportunity

to interview for a sizable position at a rival company to my last place of employment. Dear God, I hadn't been to an interview in over a decade. I had conducted more than I could count, but I had no clue how to comport myself on Zoom and regenerate that aura of calm knowledge and expertise with believable confidence. Would they be able to detect the residue of self-doubt I had tried (and not yet succeeded) to scrub away? I couldn't risk it. I enlisted my trusted friend Michael, a corporate coach, to run a few mock interviews with me. I wanted to ensure I was ready for any potential questions.

I went into prep mode as if I were preparing a case for a big trial. I researched like a madwoman and taped three-by-five index cards all over my laptop with specific facts and precise thoughts, because I tend to ramble when I get nervous. I wanted to be succinct, upbeat, protein packed.

I woke up that morning on edge. Did I want this too much? I didn't want to come across as desperate, but I wanted to convey my authentic enthusiasm. I exercised, primped a bit, and then sat down to meditate. When the interview began, I felt ready and rehearsed. It went well. I gave it my best and, despite being out of practice, felt I had left it all in the ring.

A few weeks went by and I didn't hear anything. Finally, I got a call from the company president, who told me that it had been a very tough decision, but they had decided *to go in a different direction*, and instead of hiring a person who had done the job before (me), they decided to promote an internal candidate who had been with the company for over a decade. I took the news in stride, wondering if I could have done something differently. I worked on embracing the rejection and not making it personal, but that is fucking hard. *Why not me? Why not go in my direction?*

I allowed myself to really want something and it didn't happen. These were unfamiliar waters for me. Up until now, I had succeeded in my career at getting what I wanted. If I put myself out there, it usually went my way. More new feelings to work through in therapy.

I interviewed a few more times, but nothing was panning out. Fall turned to winter and then spring, it had been eighteen months without a job. I would say my morale was at a steady low when Lilly bounced into my room and asked, "Mom, why are you sad?" But the tone felt more like, *Why are you sad NOW? Why are you sad AGAIN?* There was a veritable buffet of answers to choose from.

Hmmm, let's see. There's this one dish already heated called lack of purpose. And there's this other hot dish, withering self-esteem; another entrée, my sweet dad's impending demise; and then some spicy side dishes like recent job rejection; oh, and of course, new to the menu, lack of adult connection, with a scoop of inability to fit in or find a new community. And for dessert, looking as ugly as I feel. Where should I start?

Lilly continued, "Are you still upset about the job?" She didn't specify if it was the new one that I didn't get, the lack of a job, or that I couldn't recover from the original dismissal, which, frankly, by that point Lilly and every other person in my life deserved to ask.

I replied, "Yes, I am still sad. I want my old life back. I miss being around people. I miss jumping out of bed in the morning to have someplace to be. I miss people asking me what I think. I miss being needed."

She looked at me and tilted her head as though she was trying to figure out a puzzle. "Mom, I know you miss them, but *we* are people; *we* are your team. I miss *you*. Ozzie misses *you*. Remember when you used to dance in the kitchen?" She leaned over, kissed my cheek, then got up and left the room.

I hated this! I hated how she was seeing me. I hated that I had been so wrapped up in my gross, pathetic self. It was then that it dawned on me. The upbeat person who would bound in at the end of the day, energized and enthused to greet their faces, was MIA. Immediately I was struck with another great big reality blow: This is how they will remember me during this period of my life. The moment imprinted in their minds will be: *This is how Mom dealt with disappointment—retreat, isolation, depression, and suppressed emotions toward us.*

I was talking with my therapist a few days later, and I recounted this incident and the shame I felt for allowing my emotional hurt to permeate their young spirits. She asked, "Well, how do you want Lilly and Ozzie to remember you? What kind of lasting impressions do you want them to be left with? What will Lilly's takeaway be based on how you faced this and other big challenges in your life?"

So I thought about my parenting goals for a few days, then called back and said, "I've got it: I want them to remember their mom as having grit and determination, never running from challenges. I want to show them I confronted disappointment with grace. I want them to remember me finding humor in the irony of life and witness me leading with kindness and compassion for others but also for myself."

I thought about how we had been coexisting most recently. How could I expect Lilly and Ozzie to absorb these sentiments from me when I have only been capable of being a quarter of those desired qualities during a quarter of the last two years? Yes, there are days I still feel sad, but there are more days that I feel my worth building outside my previous definition.

Change is hard for me. My whole purpose has yet to reveal itself, but until it does, I am also learning to open myself up to the reality, and the remarkable possibility, that my mission has changed. Something I had forgotten about in my frenzied job interview prep was a much more important set of skills. My ability to infuse love, passion, and enthusiasm into the lives of the people around me, especially Lilly and Ozzie. That special skill is not listed on my LinkedIn page, but it is listed on my résumé of life. It just took a little Bird to remind me.

10

Shoeless:
Barefoot Babes in Turnaround

When I was in middle school, I attended the wedding of a family friend with my parents and sister. Seated at the reception, I watched the wedding party gather on the dance floor, the bridesmaids in their foam-green dresses of varying lengths and designs. My eyes zeroed in on a baddie, shaking her hair back and forth, followed by a full-circle head roll, as she gyrated her hips in an almost tantric motion. She was glistening in the distance with either sweat or glitter, probably both, and dancing with total abandon.

My eyes followed her head movements, then scanned down her chest and sweaty cleavage, stopping at her hips, mesmerized, then down to . . . *RECORD SCRATCH* . . . no shoes. *What the . . . ?* Why on earth was she on the dance floor in bare feet? At a wedding, no less. My brain began to short-circuit: *Is this allowed? Are her shoes too small? Can she not dance in heels?* I was spinning.

Just then the bride came into view and shimmied up to this bridesmaid with her dress lifted to mid-calf, ALSO barefoot.

This had to be some sort of dare. Why else would someone, not just someone—THE BRIDE—be on a crowded dance floor WITHOUT SHOES?

Many years later, I came to realize that boogying barefoot on a dance floor is not only common but widely accepted among women, young and old alike. Regardless of the event, there is always a girl dancing barefoot, shoes discarded nearby, or one who is leaving for the night with heels dangling from her fingers by two loose straps.

Earlier this year, Max and I attended our friends Chazz and Stu's wedding. The black-tie reception was held in a beautifully restored event space with concrete walls, high ceilings, all dripping with cascading flowers. It was so chic. There was a huge dance floor with a live drummer and a deejay. I wore hot-pink satin heels that were about a five on the comfort scale, paired with a vintage black dress. Max and I were dancing with all our friends, well past midnight. As I took a breather, I noticed no less than eight pairs of high heels lined up on the coffee table behind me, mixed between purses and jackets. In fact, orphaned designer shoes had been discarded all around the edges of the dance floor.

I have never, regardless of excruciating discomfort, taken off my shoes and walked barefoot, let alone danced, in public. I would rather wear a crop top than go without shoes. And if you knew me, you'd know that's saying a lot. I have suffered through many an event where my feet were more than a little uncomfortable, with blisters going through a whole life cycle in one evening, from bubble to burst, rather than risk nude feet.

My shoes-on rule also applies to grass and sand. Even if I walk to the ocean for a dip, I will leave my flip-flops at the tide's edge to slip back on as soon as I get out of the water. And whenever I get home from anywhere, I put my shoes back on the shelf in my closet and immediately step into my slippers. The only time slippers come off inside the house is when I step into the shower, and they go back on as soon as I step out. My bare feet do not touch the floor. When I go to bed, I place my slippers neatly nearby, ready to slide them back onto my feet come morning, until I dress for the day and put on my shoes.

Many a person has come to our house and asked upon stepping inside, "Should I take off my shoes?" to which I always respond (perhaps a little too eagerly), "Please don't." I panic when I arrive at someone's door and find out they have a shoes-off policy. I can't have a normal conversation in someone's living room or kitchen with my shoes off. Shoes put the period at the end of a sentence; without them, I feel distracted and unmoored.

Shoeless dancing to me stands for rebellion, freedom, confidence, fearlessness. I am so envious of that type of unselfconscious abandon. The archetypal barefoot girl who looms large in my imagination was raised in a house with artists, never had a curfew, and called her parents by their first names. She is sexually adventurous. She will do a shot at last call and say something like, "Fuck it, I'm taking that guy home tonight." She is feisty, like Gayle King, who Max describes as having "BIG FUN ENERGY." You *know* Gayle and Oprah at a certain point in a party cast off their shoes as they form a line to do the Wobble.

I don't consider myself tightly wound. I am not a fearful person. There are plenty of risks I have no problem taking: I will eat a chocolate mushroom or pot gummy straight from your pocket; I will drink out of your glass or borrow your spoon for a taste of dessert; I will even get in an Uber alone at one a.m., despite the wafts of weed coming from inside the car, confident I will be dropped home safely. I am not embarrassed by my feet, either—I get regular pedicures and wear open-toed shoes. So what exactly is holding me back?

This phenomenon is clearly rooted in my childhood. It goes along with my sister and me brushing our hair on Christmas morning *before* racing to see what Santa had stuffed into our stockings. We were encouraged to style our hair, put on slippers, and wear our robes over our pajamas for the *candid* photos. Later, it was suggested that "we throw on some mascara, and while you're at it, a little blush will brighten up your cheeks" for the *spontaneous* photo shoot. That is the way it was in my house growing up.

My dad was raised in a strict cleanliness-is-next-to-godliness type of home. His parents did not have money to spend on fancy clothes, but those two Sanchez boys left for school each day looking pristine, in crisply ironed clothes, with their hair perfectly combed. And my mom had her own formalities from childhood. She grew up attending ceremonious dinners and lunches with her parents, who were doctors. And both sets of my grandparents lived in uniquely rigid, dignified households. As a result, my parents never walked around our house with bare feet. In fact, I have never seen my dad wear anything but a proper shoe with laces, a loafer, or the slippers that went with his button-down pajamas and robe. I have to assume his toes have never seen daylight.

If you were looking for a casual place to hang out, it wasn't our house. There was no eating anywhere besides the kitchen table or dining room. The table was always set with place mats and place settings (usually by me), and we always wore appropriate clothing at the table, with shoes, never pajamas. It was expected by my parents and considered a sign of respect. When answering the family landline, we were taught that there was only one acceptable way to answer the phone. When I answered, I had to say, "Hello, this is Tess Sanchez speaking." My sister and I hated this so much, but we didn't really have a choice. I know—it is so cringe.

When we got older and boys began to call, we *really* protested, and finally got the rule lifted, but not until well into my sister's tenth-grade year. Once, my college roommate came to my house over Christmas break before going home to see her parents. We were chatting with my parents before dinner, and she pulled me aside: "You didn't tell me it was *fancy*."

I responded, "What are you talking about? This isn't fancy, this is normal." And by "normal," I mean my mom's look was ripped from the pages of a Talbots catalog, and my dad was straight out of Brooks Brothers, replete with a preppy silk necktie. Classical music played in the background, as the white Christmas lights mingled with the fresh cedar garlands over a warm, crackling fire. They sat drinking red wine, encouraging us to partake of the cheese plate with other canapés decorously arranged between fresh pine cones on the coffee table.

"Can I offer you a glass of champagne before dinner?" my dad asked my roommate.

Normal, right? Don't get me wrong, it wasn't exactly *Salt-burn* at my house, but the vibe was not especially casual. My roommate seemed genuinely surprised, which I took as a compliment because it meant I had not carried any trace of this formality with me to college. *See, look at me, I am casual!* I was, however, the only bridesmaid in her wedding party who still had her shoes on at the end of the night.

I remember at my sister's wedding reception there was a woman in her sixties closely related to the groom, who after taking a break from the dance floor, was sitting with her shoes off and her feet up on a chair in front of her. She fanned herself with a napkin, trying to cool down. Then out of the corner of my eye, I saw my mother walk by and stop dead in her tracks as her eyes locked on this jovial woman's bare feet. *Here we go,* I thought, picturing Meryl Streep in *The Devil Wears Prada*: "I expect a formal apology for that," pointing to her feet. But my mom kept it together and refrained. I did see something register behind her eyes, like, *Okay, stay calm, just act normal.* And in her defense, as a shoes-on tribal elder, I agree that this was not something she could have unseen.

It was clear to me from that moment on that my sister's matrimonial future was in jeopardy. You know why? Because the groom was from a family who danced with their shoes off—and aired their feet for the whole party to see. Meanwhile, my sister was raised shoes-on and grew up having to curl her hair for casual Sunday brunch at home. Sure enough, eighteen months later, a culture clash of irreconcilable differences (maybe barefoot differences) was the reason cited in the filed divorce papers. I thought about telling Christina at the wedding reception that bare feet had entered the in-law equation, but she looked so happy. I didn't want to ruin things by risking her immediate realization that this relationship didn't stand a chance.

Perhaps this should be a category on all the dating apps: Check here if you toss your shoes aside on the dance floor/check here if you would rather sustain emergency room–level blisters than be caught shoeless. It could be a very useful screening question. Obviously, the shoeless girls would be getting more action—they have BIG FUN ENERGY.

Even though I can't pull off the "barefoot girl at the wedding" myself, I can't help but be a bit spellbound by those who possess that footloose-and-fancy-free spirit. Ozzie proudly walks around our house shoeless and shirtless. His philosophy is less-is-more when it comes to clothing, regardless of weather, season, or occasion. On most mornings before he leaves the house, I'll make suggestions, but unlike me when I was his age, he will not oblige my requests.

"How about you wear sweatpants today instead of shorts. It's supposed to rain."

"No thanks."

"How about a sweatshirt?"

"No thanks. I'm good."

Lilly always kicks her shoes off the second she enters the house, and I had wondered if that carried over to her public shoe persona. We were both invited to a bar mitzvah last year and

I wondered, would she be dancing with her shoes on? Would she be in a cluster of girlfriends having the time of her life with her shoes off? This was the first year of middle school, and bar mitzvah season was in full swing. Every weekend there seemed to be another party. She wore the same black dress week after week with her Doc Marten boots, the dress, shorter than I would have preferred.

"Oh wow, you look fantastic all dressed up. I love your hair!"

"Thanks, Mama."

"Now, do you think your dress is too short?"

"No, everyone has their dress this length; besides I'm wearing shorts underneath."

"Oh, okay. As long as you feel good about it." (See? I *am* chill.)

"I feel great about it."

I remain in awe of Lilly's innate confidence. I would love to take credit for instilling the beautiful sense of self she possesses, but I don't think confidence is something you can give your child. If it were that easy to infuse, every teen girl would have it. Also, she was right about the dress. Every girl there was wearing a similar version of a very short black dress. The length looked more appropriate in a sea of micromini black dresses. Anything longer would have stood out.

I mingled with some other parents and ended up in a conversation with the mother of the boy being bar mitzvahed. After a few minutes of chatting, she grabbed my arm and said, "I love this song!" It was Beyoncé's "Break My Soul." "Come on, let's go dance." I hesitated for a moment, worried about cramping Lilly's style should we end up elbow-to-elbow on the dance floor.

But Lilly knows how I feel about Bey—there is no holding me back when it comes to the Queen. "Let's go," I said, following her into the fray.

We were dancing and feeling it when I heard, "Mom, watch!" I spun around, and who do I see with both hands in the air, dancing with shoeless abandon on the dance floor? My very own flesh and blood. I smiled at her. *She is so free*, I thought contentedly. Just then, Lilly dropped to the floor and did the Worm across the filthy dance floor, as a group of friends cheered her on. She popped back up onto her bare feet and proudly looked back to see if I had watched. I gave her a big smile and a thumbs-up.

It reminded me of a story Max had told me about himself at thirteen years old. He would spend hours in the corner of an adult party doing the Running Man until he was drenched in sweat. He wouldn't even take a break when an adult came over to chat with him. He would just keep doing the dance, like it was his job. This vision has always stuck in my mind. This and the photos he'd shown me from his own *SNL*-themed bar mitzvah. Each table at his party was themed with a different character—Gumby, the Coneheads, Church Lady, Wayne Campbell of *Wayne's World*, Matt Foley, Mazel Maxie.

Now we'd come full circle, with Lilly worming her way across the floor, fully committed, with the same amount of fervor Max had at that age. So, my question was answered: no shoes necessary. Lilly took home a prize that night for being *the most lit on the dance floor*. She did the Worm like it was her job, earning every dollar of the Starbucks gift card.

Despite inheriting a certain conditioned formality from my

parents that I find impossible to shake, I am so proud that I did not pass my rigid policy along to Lilly or Ozzie. What we as parents can't fully embrace in our lives, we can only hope our kids have the option to choose in theirs. I accept and celebrate the freedoms others enjoy; I just choose to do all these things in the comfort of my Nike trainers.

But now I find myself wondering, *Is this about more than shoes and feet? Am I truly the epitome of propriety? Am I forever choosing formality over casual abandon?* My conundrum is that I want a foot in both camps, as it were. I would love to kick off my shoes and dance with exuberant freedom, but I know I wouldn't feel like me. If I really dig deep, maybe it's about judgment from others?

Life is littered with battles between formality and informality. Take cloth versus paper napkins, for example. Just the other day, I asked Lilly to set the table for dinner for our family and Chazz and Stu, who were joining us. As she put down the six place mats, plates, and silverware, I saw her carefully folding six paper towels and placing them under each fork.

"What are you doing?" I asked.

"I'm setting the table," she said.

"Right, but the napkins are in the side table. The cloth napkins?"

"Mom, no one cares about cloth napkins except you."

I thought to myself, *Is that true?* Perhaps. But when I spent more time really thinking about it, I concluded that putting thought and effort into our guests' dining experience is what matters to me. A nice place setting reflects that I care about someone and want them to enjoy their meal in our home. Wait: *Are cloth napkins my love language?* Now *that* is a concept I can really get behind. Maybe the somewhat stodgy traditions ingrained in my DNA are just splinters of the love language my parents passed on to me.

My mom insisted we handwrite thank-you notes on stationery for every gift we ever received, to express our gratitude. I didn't love writing those thank-you notes at the time, but look at me now. Today, I insist Lilly and Ozzie do the same for family members who send gifts or host us at their house. It's not that I don't love receiving a text from a friend saying, "OMG, great party last night. Thx. UR the OG." Honestly, it's sometimes too enticing and labor-saving to resist sending a text myself. But a handwritten note on thick cardstock is so much more special. Hold on. *Are handwritten notes also my love language?*

This got me thinking: *Is this whole shoes-off ethos not so much a question of rules versus rebellion, but something more subtle?* Although I was raised in a shoes-on, cloth-napkin-using, handwritten-note-sending household, that doesn't mean everyone shares my love language. My shoes-on philosophy may reflect my preference for stability, with each step measured and predictable, safe and secure, on a well-paved road. But ahh, how I sometimes long to be the shoes-off adventurer, dashing off thank-you texts, standing at the kitchen counter holding a drumstick and wiping my mouth with a paper towel. If I can just accept who I am while enjoying other people's idiosyncrasies, maybe that's the secret to embracing the uncertainty that has been dogging me ever since my life circumstances changed.

That night, we sat for a family dinner with Chazz and Stu and used paper towels for napkins. Lilly was right, no one cared. The conversation was rich, the laughs were plenty, and I was fortified by the sweet company. The quality of any experience is about the people, and while I still appreciate shoes, cloth napkins, and thank-you notes, they have no bearing on the real connections we are meant to share.

The next day, I received a text from Chazz that read: "Thank U for having us last night. So fun to hang, really needed those LOLs."

The defense rests.

11

Cycle of Life:
Syndication

After months in pandemic lockdown, I was finally able to visit my parents, who lived about a two-hour drive from us. While it was such a relief to see them in person again, I wasn't prepared for the version of my dad that greeted me. Much older, thinner, and frail, having lost about twenty pounds from an already trim frame. His posture had changed, too: His bones seemed to curl inward as he adopted a more cautious, hunched gait. His once-gorgeous skin had become dry and ashy with veins showing through, and was sprinkled with age spots. It was honestly a bit shocking. How had I missed all of this on our Zoom calls? The only word that comes to mind is "decay," closely accompanied by the thought: *WHY?* Why does this horrid disease of the mind also have to erode his physical body, too?

In the sixteen months since my father's diagnosis, it was clear that the isolation of the pandemic had accelerated his illness. As I spent time with him that weekend, I would stare into his eyes, wondering and worrying about what was going on in his brain. Sometimes he seemed very aware of his surroundings, but at other times he was unresponsive, staring off into the distance, not even nodding his head yes or no. I wondered whether he understood my words, or if it sounded like I was speaking in a foreign language.

Each morning, he would pretend to read *The New York Times*, holding the paper in front of him, but his eyes fixed in one place, not moving. He pretended to watch the news, too, but again it appeared as though he was just staring at the TV and not digesting any information. I couldn't decipher exactly which disease—aphasia or Alzheimer's—was robbing which function.

He had always played our beautiful Steinway piano and had been able to read sheet music with ease, but sometime during this downhill spiral, he just stopped playing. I don't know if it was his finger mobility or an inability to read the notes on the page. And he certainly couldn't explain why. One day the music just stopped.

As my sweet Ozzie was learning how to read, my dad slowly, and then quickly, became unable to. I watched as my son transformed from baby to boy, just as I witnessed my dad becoming more dependent and toddler-like. My father's life now, from my perspective, consisted of having his basic needs met: *Are you hungry? Are you tired? Are you cold? Are you hot? Do you want to sit outside or inside?* This ultimate paternal figure now relied on other people to provide and care for him.

The dismantling of his freedom did not happen overnight. Initially, he had put up much more of a fight. When the doctor asked him early on, "Do you understand what I am saying? You have Alzheimer's," my dad nodded in recognition so clearly, we were sure that he did, in fact, understand. Slowly, that look of recognition became fainter and fainter, and confusion started to set in.

The first clear incident occurred when he called a jewelry store to order a necklace for my mom for Valentine's Day. He'd spent time on the phone mumbling to the saleswoman on the other end, and eventually tried to pay with his credit card. With the strained communication, the saleswoman did not get the credit card numbers correct and told my dad the card had been declined. He was convinced that my sister and I had canceled his card, which we hadn't. In fact, we did not even have power of attorney had we wanted to intervene. He was holding on tightly to every shred of independence he still had.

The hardest turning point came a year after his initial diagnosis, when my dad was left alone at the house and he decided to drive himself to the grocery store a mile and a half away, to buy orange juice and milk. He had driven that same route hundreds of times before. He parked in this mega strip mall that housed a grocery store, a pharmacy, fast-food restaurants, and a couple of random little shops. After walking out of the grocery store, having purchased nothing, he went to find his car. He searched and searched but couldn't remember where he'd parked. It became dark while he was roaming around the parking lot alone.

My dad had his cell phone with him but couldn't remember how to use it. And then he spotted a T-Mobile store and went in and handed his phone to the clerk. With the progressing aphasia, he was unable to tell the salesclerk what was happening. The clerk opened the phone, and through some sort of prompting from my dad, managed to call my mom and say, "Your husband is here. I think he wanted me to call you."

He had been gone for over an hour. Panicked, my mom jumped into an Uber to pick him up, and then drove them home in his car, which was parked right in front of the market where he had left it. My heart broke when my mom told me about this episode. How scared he must have felt, alone in the dark, lost. This worldly man who has lived and traveled abroad and navigated foreign countries with cool confidence had just gotten lost in a parking lot a mile and a half from his home.

We all agreed it was no longer safe for him to drive. As his car keys quietly slipped out of sight, next came his cell phone, and then his credit cards. It was awful. I have witnessed all these small things, and then larger things, taken away from my dad like a trickle and then a flood, and felt how devastating this all must have been for such a fiercely independent man. My mom obviously had it the worst, being with him twenty-four seven and enforcing the limited access and restrictions we had put in place for him. My dad would grow angry, taking it out on her by icing her out; he would ignore her for days and refuse to engage.

Ironically, the old Sanchez ice-out was how we all historically handled conflict and disappointment in my family, even without illness. No yelling or raised voices. The philosophy was, why bother communicating openly and honestly when you can stomp around and stew on something for days? As an adult, I have learned (from experience) that avoiding conflict does not make the conflict go away or provide an opportunity for feelings about the conflict to evolve. All those emotions we stuff down need to find their way out, otherwise they will rot our insides. After witnessing the erosion of my dad's vocabulary, I especially appreciate the great privilege it is to have words and the ability to tell another person how you feel and why. It's a great reminder to never take the ability to use your voice for granted.

As his illness progressed, the familial roles shifted again. My sister and I took a more parental position with both Mom and Dad, a dynamic that all four of us found deeply uncomfortable to navigate. And as time marched relentlessly on, and the care of my dad became much more complex, we approached my mom about moving into a more supportive living situation. I pointed out that the upkeep on their house was far too time-consuming, with too many details to manage. And wouldn't she rather spend time walking on the beach with Dad, going out to breakfast, and enjoying these years in a more peaceful, simple way?

This is when I gained the valuable experience of what it will be like to negotiate with teenage Lilly and Ozzie. They pushed back, standing their ground, providing evidence to make their case. "Nope, we're not ready. We're good. We like living here." Mom went on, noting her sound judgment and independence, "In fact, a very nice guy just stopped by who was selling solar panels. I purchased the entire system consisting of eight panels to be installed on the roof next week. It's going to save energy, and money. The salesman was so friendly, I wrote the check right then and there."

Umm, Houston . . . we have a problem.

"What's the name of the company? How much do they charge? What happens to your existing roof? Are they licensed? Or vetted?" Will this installation actually happen?

What was even more alarming than a traveling salesman selling solar panels and my mom's fandom for him, was the lack of duress my mom was feigning. Look, we all have different coping mechanisms, and my mom chose the route of denial. Every time I spoke with her, she was giving a Blythe Danner–level performance of how fantastic things were going. It was so suspect.

"Hi Mom."

"Oh, hi Tess. Let me get Dad on the phone, too. Pablo, say hi to Tess."

"Hello?" he whispered.

"Hi Dad. How are you guys?"

"FABULOUS!" my mother would chime in. "It's a beautiful day here. We got up, took a walk, and sat down for breakfast. Later, we are having the Resniks over for lunch in the backyard—all ten feet apart, of course. And tomorrow we are going to hear an outdoor concert in Balboa Park. We are very busy—right, Pablo?"

Silence. She would continue—*blah, blah, blah*—not missing a beat. It was biz as usual for Mrs. Sanchez—a healthy calendar of social activities, excursions, and never an acknowledgment of sadness or recognition of where this disease would be taking him. It was almost as if she thought this was just a phase he was going to grow out of. That type of commitment to an alternate reality and outcome was Oscar-worthy.

Finally, I was able to convince them to at least allow me to hire a full-time home health aide, who would help shower and dress my dad, buy groceries, and cook. After about three months with this added support in place, I drove down for a visit and found no less than fifty Post-it Notes in and around my mom's desk with dates, passwords, and phone numbers. There were stacks of bills and insurance statements. I was instantly reminded of Russell Crowe in *A Beautiful Mind. What is all this information, and how does any of this make sense?* When I dug further, I discovered delinquent, unpaid cable and utility bills.

My mom had become CEO of their life, and it appeared the job had become too big to manage. In the past, this had been a two-person job, with each person having a separate calendar, with systems in place to organize bills and tasks. On top of the added administrative duties, she was now responsible for my father's medical appointments, paperwork, medications, speech therapy, dental appointments, haircuts, as well as her own. It was just too much. That night I spent six hours organizing, shredding, alphabetizing, color-coding, and putting systems in place for paperless, automatic everything. Even after pulling an organizing all-nighter and creating a master calendar, I knew the situation was untenable.

It was time. Christina and I insisted that my parents move someplace where they both could get help. I hated every minute of this role, but we had to intervene.

I began with, "We need to get you out of this house to a place with more support."

Christina chimed in: "Yes, it is really time."

My mom wasn't having it. "No, we love it here. We are never moving. Why would we? Everything is going so well."

I persisted. "Let's just check out some senior communities. I'll go with you."

"I don't think so."

"Let's just see what is even available. The waiting list could take a year."

Christina offered, "Mom, let's just start the process; you may fall in love with a place."

Mom finally relented. "Fine. I will agree to look, nothing more."

Thank God for my sister, who quickly booked tours of several facilities (all referred to in their brochures as *gorgeous senior communities*).

Again, I pitched to my mom, "Isn't it going to be such a relief not to have to worry about all the upkeep of this house? You'll get to hang out with Dad and plan fun things to do together. I think Dad really needs more planned activities."

And to my dad, I would lean over, appealing to his business side, and say, "Oh, Dad, Mom is letting stuff go. I found a delinquent utility bill. You have to go along with this move— she is just so disorganized," to which he actually giggled and nodded in agreement. Ever the provider, it was almost as if he were saying, *Yes, I will agree to move because your mom needs the help.* My strategy eventually worked, and they both got on board. Sorta.

I listened and learned a lot on those *gorgeous senior community* tours about the different levels of care available—independent, assisted, and memory care, and how they accommodate partners who need less care and can live on their own. I also demonstrated some of my finest acting, expressing only enthusiasm and excitement for each facility, providing a positive spin, and citing all the incredible features each place had to offer: "They have happy hour every day from four to six p.m.? Sign me up!" "You can walk two blocks to one of your favorite restaurants? How great is that?" "Oh my God, room service?! Can I move in?" That was *my* Oscar-worthy performance.

One place was small, with oceanfront views, where most occupants sat all day long on their balconies, gazing at the sea. It seemed peaceful but lacked any sense of community and did not have organized group activities. Somewhat isolated, it was more of an apartment complex exclusively for old people.

There was the high-rise, a sexy Manhattan-style setup with a doorman and valet parking, but most of the units did not have kitchens, and meals had to be eaten in the main dining room. *Isn't that technically a hotel?* This place also had a luxury bus with tinted windows that packed 'em in for a day at the museums or a matinee movie or play. They even had outings to the symphony.

A TV writer friend of mine was developing a show about an old-age home and had visited several facilities in Los Angeles for research. He was surprised to learn that retirement communities have the highest rates for spreading STDs. They can't be bothered to wear condoms and have given up any pretense. This place in particular had a lot of single elders and sounded like hook-up central. Also, now that marijuana was legal in California, they took edibles and got their party on.

Another place felt like an artificial movie set, much like *The Truman Show*. When we toured this site, which was part of a chain of communities in other cities, they were having some kind of sales seminar or work retreat with about thirty employees straight out of hospitality school brainstorming ways to think *outside the box* about exceptional service. Every question I asked, they answered, "Yes, we can do that. Yes, I am sure we can accommodate that. Pets? No problem. Did I offer you water? Can I get you a coffee? Just sign here and we'll get you all settled." I looked at my mom. "This place looks so great. Right?"

A few places had memory care units. I could not help equating them with the day care that Lilly and Ozzie had attended— the marked difference being that Lilly and Ozzie would graduate to preschool and kindergarten and on to bigger adventures in life. These places were not a stop; they were a destination. Like the day care baby brigade, with high chairs all lined up for their mealtimes, these units had the same setup. The nurses spoke with the same elevated volume and overpronunciation of simple words: "HOW ARE YOU TODAY, SYLVIA?" Sylvia would smile and nod and look down at her plate. One gentleman was being fed mushy food by an aide with a spoon delivered straight into his mouth. *Here comes the airplane!*

No matter how well-decorated, how ideally located, or how outfitted with amenities like ocean views, indoor pools, or fun movie nights, it was all depressing to me. I could not have imagined my parents living in any of these places. I was scared to endorse any of them for fear they would hate it and blame me. There was something in the quietness of the halls that was haunting. But despite my doubts, we had to press on.

This was a downsizing not only of their physical environment but of their entire world. Their house and their backyard were where I wanted to remember them. But my mom could no longer physically handle moving my dad's rigid body around their two-story home; the pure physicality of it was wearing on her small frame. Despite having someone there around the clock, it was still not enough.

Finally, after all the tours were complete, my sister and I met with our parents to give careful consideration to the variety of options. We made a list of pros and cons for each place and insisted they pick one. My mom and dad decided on a place that split the difference between them all: independent, near the ocean, lots of classes, nice views, a regular air-conditioned van for transport to activities and appointments, and the residents were predominantly couples. Relieved, I picked up the phone to let the facility know we had selected their community, only to find out that there was a long and involved application process. *Wait . . . we have to AUDITION to give you money for an apartment we won't own?* That's right!

Thirty pages of paperwork, with doctor sign-offs, two in-person interviews plus cognitive tests, and—how could I forget—a veterinary sign-off and interview for their dog, Sophie. An application for NASA was less complicated than this. I quickly found out it was more competitive than applying for an Ivy League college. And just like applying for a job, I swear they can smell when you're desperate. We worked for months trying to get the paperwork completed and filed.

Turning the full force of my need for a project to this endeavor was not at all how I'd seen my year going. I would happily go back to wrangling Lilly and Ozzie through Zoom school. Wrangling my own parents was an entirely different ball game. On more than one occasion during these months, my mom would call me and say, "I've changed my mind. I think we'll just stay in the house and not move after all." *Oh no, no, no, lady. We are going to see this through.* After all this, I was determined to get my parents accepted in this place. It was game on, and my competitive instincts came into focus.

I would explain, "We are so close. If for some crazy reason we don't get in, then we can talk about you staying. Let's just see what happens." At one point, my mom even emailed the head admissions guy and asked to pull their application because they had decided to stay in their house. That was the only time during this whole process that my sister completely lost it. She called me and was yelling so loud into the phone, Max could hear her as he walked beside me. This was a level-ten freak-out.

"Un-fucking-believable! She went fucking rogue!"

"What? Who? What are you talking about?"

"Mom emailed Mark at 4:30 a.m. and said that she and Dad have decided not to move. After everything we have done to get to this place, how could she do this?"

"She is clearly terrified. Take a breath. I'll call Mark right now and tell him that the email was a mistake. We can save this. Then I'll call Mom."

"I can't; I just CANNOT!"

"I'll call you back after I get this back on track."

I immediately called the head of admissions (think Mark Consuelos) and told him that my mother was just nervous about the test, that of course we wanted to proceed. Then I called my mom and calmly talked her through the importance of the move, reminding her that we had made this decision together and if they hated it, we would move them out.

"It's not prison, and this is not a sentencing. You can come and go as you please. We will keep your house so you will always have a place to go," I reassured her.

"It's not about that; it's about the test," she finally confessed. "I have a master's degree in education from Boston University, but if I miss more than five answers, it is considered a failure, and your dad and I can't move in. I have such anxiety about it. My friend Beverly just took this test to get into Piper Sands and she didn't pass. Now she has to move into the apartments down the street."

"Mom, I get it. You know what the best strategy to combat nerves is? Preparation, preparation, preparation. Let's get you ready so you feel confident. We have a month. You can do this."

I hung up the phone and turned to Max. "How do I score a copy of an old-age-home cognitive test? I need it for my mom."

"Isn't that cheating?" he asked.

"No. Maybe? I don't know. And honestly, Max, I don't give a fuck. The stakes are too high. She *has* to pass the test. *We* have to pass this test." I thought perhaps I should hire an SAT-prep type of tutor, but for seniors. Do those exist? Good business idea. Maybe that should be my next job.

It was time for me to get crafty. The next day I called her primary care physician's office and inquired if they knew what might be on such a test. They said the test was pretty standard, but they didn't have a copy. So I turned to where any person of my generation would turn to for help and real answers—Google. In the words of my girl Britney Spears, *ding dang y'all*, I found it. It's referred to as a MoCA test. The Montreal Cognitive Assessment, a 30-point early screening test for mild cognitive impairment. After printing it and reading it over a few times, out came my trusty three-by-five index cards.

I wrote out each question on the front, with the answer on the back. "Count backward from 100 in increments of seven." Another one was: "I am going to say twenty words, how many can you repeat by memory?" Some basic math word problems: "Draw a clock that says 11:30." There were some geography questions, some current affairs as well. It wasn't *not* tricky. She was going to have to memorize these answers. I mailed her an envelope with the finished flash cards.

My sister was visiting when the cards arrived a few days later. I called her: "You have to start studying with Mom; go over them every day. Morning and evening, thirty-minute study sessions."

"I'm on it," Christina said.

I set a date two weeks prior to the actual test for a pretend interview and test. Every day I called my mom: "Are you studying?"

"Oh yes," she assured me.

"Okay, Mom, calling you now on FaceTime for your pretend test." We got through four questions and the rest were a disaster. I remained calm, but inside I was panicked. I tried to sound encouraging but wrapped the call and went to find Max.

"I need your help," I said. "Can you figure out how to sync my mom's hearing aid with her iPhone?"

"I don't know. Why?"

"I'm worried about her cognitive test. If you can sync up the hearing aid, I can hear the questions in real time and feed her the answers through the phone, which will be in her purse."

"Tess, you can't game the system to get your parents in, and also, the iPhone-in-her-purse idea would never work," Max said.

"What, you think I'm the first person to give an applicant a leg up? This is not a Lori Loughlin/Varsity Blues type of situation. I am not lying about my mom being on a rowing team to get her into USC. This is an elderly woman needing a little extra edge to ensure she passes a silly test."

"Well, I am not going to jail over this admissions scandal, part two, the senior edition."

"So you are not going to help me? Fine. I'll figure this out on my own."

I was not going to let this go. I was going to do what I had to do to get her to pass this test. If she could just remain level-headed, I knew we had a shot.

As the test day approached, I continued to build my mom's confidence, encouraging her to keep studying. Maybe a Xanax for her (and one for me) the day of the test? Yes, definitely.

The next day, my sister and I dropped her off at the office and met the warm and chatty nurse who would be administering the test. We also stopped by to say hi to "Mark" and deliver a basket of muffins and pastries from a local French bakery. I know . . . shameless, but at least it wasn't an envelope of cash.

We were lip glossed and had on display our brightest smiles and attitudes. Don't you want the fun, flirty Sanchez sisters to be the enjoyable relatives of your new tenants? Mark was really gracious . . . and flirty right back. No wedding ring . . . *hmmm.* I had met him before, but I was now seeing him with a new set of eyes.

Mark was the one person standing between my parents having a dream place to live out their final years. *Shit, I am going to have to sleep with him in order to get my parents accepted into this establishment, aren't I? I am sure Max would understand. I did say I would do anything to make this happen. A fun romp in exchange for a move-in date? People have boned for less worthy reasons.*

We picked my mom up two hours later. "Well?"

"I think it went well," she assured us.

We went back to the house and waited . . . and waited.

At about four p.m., Mark called and asked that we all return to his office for a meeting. *Why?* I wondered. *Why can't you just tell us over the phone? Why do we have to go in?* Like a trip to Sunday mass, my sister, my parents, and I filed into the car together. This was the moment of truth. Everything we had been working toward over the last four months. I wanted this so bad I could taste it. There was no version of rejection that I was going to be able to digest. I envisioned tearing apart their office if it was anything but yes. I was on the edge of hysteria. My family needed this win, this victory. *Just say yes!*

We entered and sat around a big wood conference table. Mark and two other male administrators joined him. They looked serious. "We reviewed your test. In order to move in and qualify for independent living, you needed a combined score of 90 or above. Mrs. Sanchez, you scored 89.5, which we will consider a 90. Congratulations, and welcome to Piper Sands."

I jumped to my feet and hugged my mom. "You did it. I knew you could."

On the eve of their move-in date, thoughts of how I would walk away from their new home that very first time ran through my head. I'd never imagined my life going in that direction. Scheming like an *Ocean's Eleven* plot to get my parents accepted. Being stuck in the middle as the very people you love the most— your children and your parents—go through a sort of cosmic Benjamin Button–esque swap really makes you reprioritize what matters. Like how grateful I was for Google, and for the grading system that generously gave an additional half a point. And that I didn't have to break my marriage vows during the application process.

12

The Plus-One Era:
N/I (as in, Not Interested)

Max has always dreamt of visiting a dude ranch. He's a Jew from New York with definite cowboy envy.

Now, I'm not opposed to a getaway filled with outdoor activities, but at this particular moment, when I was questioning my own self-worth and generally having an identity crisis, I was feeling especially triggered by all things related to traditional male archetypes. Unlike past vacations, where the four of us were reconnecting away from our busy lives, this trip was happening after twenty months of being together *all* the time. The idea of wide-open plains as far as the eye could see trumped any reservations I may have had. This trip was Max's dream, so he made all the travel arrangements. We just came along to support his cowboy fantasies.

When Max and I met, and during the first ten years of our relationship, he was my plus-one. Tess Sanchez's plus-one boyfriend, then husband. I always made the travel arrangements, because I was making the money mostly. I still make all our travel arrangements, because I'm good at it, and also a bit of a control freak. We would check into hotels, and they would refer to Max as Mr. Sanchez, which always made me smile. I received the invites, we followed my social calendar, and I was the conversation starter who took up the space in the room. But right then, I was (in my mind) at my most uninteresting, the least like my old self. I felt as though I had nothing to bring to the table—literally nothing. *Me*, Tess Sanchez, with nothing to say? I had lost all my connective tissue to the world and the people in it.

I had always considered myself skilled at talking with people, at finding common ground, asking questions, and listening. But I could no longer tap into that. Now it was more like, "So, how about that rain? Crazy, right?" Even *I* wanted to walk away from conversations with the person I had become.

I had become BORING. There. I said it. The dirtiest word in my vocabulary. Call me a tasteless ding-dong, call me *anything* else, but do not call me boring. When Max sends me flowers, his notes now include affirmations like: "I am obsessed with your sensational personality. I love you!" He knows me so well that he realizes these are the only compliments that turn me on.

We were greeted at the airport in Montana by a silver-haired gentleman holding a sign that read MAX GREENFIELD PARTY. *Ugh*. I guess we are the party to one Max Greenfield. I know it shouldn't bother me, but after everything, it really got under my skin. Why not, WELCOME, SANCHEZ-GREENFIELD FAMILY?

We piled into the van and were completely blown away by the breathtaking scenery. The sky was so blue; the air felt so fresh and clean. The clouds resembled fake, floating marshmallows.

Every lush shade of green surrounded us, with snow-capped mountains in the distance. After a thirty-minute drive, I felt a little bit better as we pulled onto a winding road to the resort and filed out of the car and into a lobby filled with fresh-faced college kids, all clearly working their summer jobs.

The staff was lovely and kind . . . and solely focused on *Mr. Greenfield*. It had been a while since we'd been around Max the Actor. In fact, Ozzie had been locked inside for so long that he was completely perplexed by a breathless young male staff member (think Jared Hess) who appeared in front of us as we walked out of the reception area. He was holding a tiny pad of yellow Post-it Notes, and he asked Max for his autograph. *Seriously? On a Post-it Note? O-kay.*

Max happily scratched out his name on two separate notes, one for breathless Napoleon Dynamite and one for Napoleon's friend. I had to remind myself that we were not in Los Angeles or New York, where people don't bat an eye at Max. I forgot that, after years of scanning through headshots, I'm a bit more immune to celebrity than most at this point, but God bless the kind people of Montana who acted as if Tom Cruise had arrived.

Ozzie, confused, asked, "Why does he want Dad's autograph?"

Irked, I responded, "I think they are confusing Dad with someone else."

We checked into our cabin to find gift baskets of wine and chocolate, mugs, T-shirts, all addressed to Mr. Greenfield— and only Mr. Greenfield. At our first breakfast, as soon as we sat down, the waitress (think Vanessa Bayer) approached with her coffeepot. Smiling broadly and gazing into Max's eyes, she poured his coffee and asked how his first night was, then walked away.

"Um, excuse me . . . miss?" I said. "May I have . . ."

Nope, she was gone.

She returned ten minutes later, thank God, but only to ask Max, "Can I top you off?"

I blurted out, "Huuunnnney, I would love some coffee too."

She turned to me, startled, as though seeing me for the first time. "Of course," she mumbled. My internal reply was something along the lines of *Girl, wake up!* Instead, I smiled and replied, "Thank you so much."

Ozzie was totally amazed by these fawning strangers, as guest after guest approached: "I never do this, I am so sorry to interrupt, but my [fill in the blank] is your biggest fan. Can I get a picture?" At which point, they would thrust their cell phone into my hand and snuggle up for their photo. *Don't you worry! This faceless, nameless lady is always happy to take the picture.*

What became increasingly clear was that *New Girl* had taken on an enormous new audience on Netflix during the pandemic. The comments just kept coming: "You got us through quarantine." "I binged *New Girl*, like, three times in a row, all seven seasons." Even during the height of the show's success, it had not been like this. Or had I just never noticed because I had my own life and identity? I began to feel as though I were just a nonspeaking extra in the background.

I suppose we were vacationing with the show's exact demographic audience—we were in the middle of the country at a dude ranch filled with families and college-aged staff. Even Lilly was getting noticed from the homeschool videos she and Max had done together. Do I need to get blonder highlights or something?

But in that gorgeous environment, we were easily coaxed into having fun. Mostly. Ozzie had the body of a five-year-old, but the outdoor experience of a three-year-old after quarantining in our suburban neighborhood for two years. Some of the activities offered were exciting in theory, but the reality of a trail ride was a different story. Any trail ride I have ever been on with children has gone awry more often than not, and this one proved no exception.

It was raining and cold, and Ozzie's horse, Butterscotch, a big and sturdy battle-axe of an animal, wanted to go back to the barn and demanded that Ozzie go with him. When I turned around to check on Ozzie, his horse promptly made a tight U-turn and began trotting away from us toward the barn. Ozzie was holding onto the reins for dear life as his feet popped out of the stirrups. All I saw was the back of his little helmet and his bright yellow poncho bouncing up and down, accompanied by his shrieks of terror fading into the distance.

The guide, a badass lady cowboy ("cowlady" just doesn't sound right), galloped after him and brought the horse back, with Ozzie still in the saddle. He sobbed, "I don't like this; I don't like this. Mom, please make this stop." I do believe in the saying that if you don't get right back on the horse, you never will, so I insisted he was a hero, and we continued the ride. Meanwhile, Lilly's priority was not her brother's safety but rather getting the right photos of herself as she posed atop her horse taking selfies. Ah, the city slickers.

We completed the trail ride, and I was pretty sure Ozzie would never get on a horse again. Perhaps one day he will be able to wear this ride as a badge of bravery, unless I have scarred him for the foreseeable future. We were those resort parents who torture their kids by throwing them into terrifying activities while gritting our teeth. "You'll learn to LOVE nature, goddamnit." Conversely, Lilly was all, "Loving it, guys! Namaste."

Upon checking us in for our white-water-rafting activity, the guide (think Merritt Wever) looked at her clipboard. "Mr. Greenfield, Ms. Sanchez, right this way to the boat." Max had registered me under my name, as we always did. It had never occurred to me to change my name when we got married. I felt a strong sense of self and a deep connection to my Latin roots. Changing my name to Tess Greenfield was not on the table, and Max totally got that.

As we were loading up the boat and putting on life jackets, the guide leaned in and asked, "Do you get to travel with the Greenfields often?"

Say what? I was so taken aback by the question that I said the first thing that came to mind: "Only when they ask me to."

Okay, so there are a few things to dig into here: (1) It did not occur to "Merritt" that a woman (me) would keep her own name when she married—more than a little *Handmaid's Tale*, if you ask me. At least she didn't call me "Ofmax"; (2) "*Get to*" travel with them? The implied assumption is that with a Latin name like Ms. Sanchez, it must mean that I *worked for* the

Greenfields, right? This sent shock waves up my spine. Wow!
Okay, so not a lot of diversity around these parts. Say it three
times: *Tess: We are not in a big city. We are not in a big city. We
are not in a big city*; (3) Do these children not look like me?;
and (4) What year is it?!

As we settled into the boat wearing our helmets and layers
of clothes over our bathing suits, Ozzie reminded Max and me
that he DID NOT WANT to go rafting. It was early June, and
the river water was around fifty degrees. We reassured him that
it would be fun, and we headed toward the rapids. As we pushed
off, freezing water began sloshing into the boat—at first, splash-
ing Ozzie's legs, then his arms, but when it started hitting him in
the face, he finally reached his limit. He grabbed my hand and
leg, folded his body toward me, and let out the loudest, shrillest
screams of "Mommmmmmmy, Mommy, Mommy!"

I responded with words of warmth and comfort. When those
words failed, I tried to distract him by pointing out various natural wonders around us. But Ozzie wasn't having it. He continued
to cry at a level ten for the full forty-five-minute journey. Finally,
as we exited the boat, everyone's nerves were a little frayed,
but I couldn't resist. I looked back at our guide and casually
said, "I make the children call me Mommy." Merritt looked so
confused and embarrassed, clearly under the impression that
Mr. Greenfield was banging the help.

On to the go-kart racing, which was Ozzie's dream, and the
least nature-filled activity offered. I did some laps in the tiny box
car and then stood off the track, watching the kids transfused
with glee at each being in their own race car, tearing around the

corners of the track. The thought struck me that we didn't need to be in Montana for this, as there is a similar place in Burbank just twenty minutes from our house, but . . . fine. I just wanted them to have fun.

As I stood there delighting in their glee, the young female course attendant sidled up to me. "How long have you been with the Greenfield family?" *Seriously?* I played along and told her it had been about ten years. She carried on, "They seem really nice." *YES, GIRL, WE ARE.*

At lunch that day, I told the kids and Max about the mix-up about my perceived role in the family. Ozzie said, "Wait, they think you're our nanny, not our mom?" They all burst out laughing, thinking it was the funniest thing they had ever heard. Sigh.

Let me be crystal clear, this mistaken identity bullshit had never happened before. I had always held my own space. Why now? Was I carrying myself differently? Around every corner was another person shoving a cell phone in my face to take their picture with Max. I think my dismay started to become apparent as one lady looked at me with pity and offered, "Do you want to be in the picture too?" *No, sweetie, I'm good.*

Since this was Max's trip, and we wanted to acknowledge his effort in planning it, we all hung in there with the required attitude adjustment and persevered with the scheduled activities he had carefully planned. Next stop, the ropes course. With another family, we took seats in a big van and headed to a remote part of the property.

This child-safe course included a twenty-minute safety lesson on how to clip in your harness and scale a rope between two trees. Concerned that either or both kids might have a panic attack dozens of feet above the ground, my best and only strategy was, *Don't look down*. We all cautiously proceeded up the ladder to the first platform. As the kids became more comfortable, their confidence grew, and before we knew it, we three had left Max far behind. We reached the end with a grand finale, a fifty-foot drop to a platform on the ground. Despite being fully harnessed with safety gear, including a helmet, Max remained on the elevated platform, immobile for thirty minutes. Even after seeing us—including Ozzie—jump down, he couldn't move.

As the sun began to set, the other family and guide had long packed up and left us behind. A single guide and an additional van patiently waited to return us to base camp. We cheered Max on with words of encouragement: "Come on, Max!" "You've got this, Dad!" For a minute, I almost thought it was an act Max was performing to make Ozzie feel better about being overly cautious with the previous activities. I started to film this unbelievable scene, laughing so hard I had tears streaming down my face. Max continued to sit in a tree, shaking his head and muttering, "I can't do it."

Lilly came to me and said, "Mom, stop laughing. Dad is really scared." But it was too late, I had the giggles. I think all the stress and internal dialogue were just erupting out of me. Eventually, the guide had to impose a time limit and said, "Max, there's one other way down. I'll come up and get you."

Max wore a look of humiliation as he backed down a rope ladder that had been hidden in the trees, followed by complete silence in the van on the way back to the lodge. As our guide, a patient and sensible outdoors lady (think Cherry Jones) stopped the car, she turned to us and in a hushed tone said, "You know, what happens at the ropes course stays at the ropes course."

I could not help but enjoy this. Max is so good at everything. He is supremely athletic, fearless in any ocean. He runs a yearly triathlon. Even his Ping-Pong game is unmatched. To witness him sulking in defeat, pouting as if he had just lost his spot qualifying for the Olympics, was something I had not seen before.

I tried to offer my genuine support, but I couldn't deliver it with a straight face. Yes, he had to climb down the "loser ladder," as he called it. *Big deal*, I thought. *Let's talk about real humiliation that is my current life, the kind I am swimming around in daily.* I gave him an hour to shake it off, at which point he announced we would be returning to the ropes course. I knew before he even said it, this family was never going to make it out of Montana without Max conquering that jump. For God's sake, a man's ego was at stake here!

We returned to the ropes course the next day, and the three of us cheered him on once again. And who was manning the course that day? None other than Cherry Jones from the day before. "Hello, Max and family. Max, are you ready to face your fears?" she asked with an earnest look in her eye.

He climbed to the top of the platform, joined by Cherry, who, before he could think too long about it, gave him a gentle shove. Descending in almost slow motion, he floated down, belaying to the cushy mat below. VICTORY! He stood, as Ozzie, Lilly, and I all applauded. Raising his hand, he shook his head, acknowledging that the slow-motion decent was in fact rather comical and not scary at all. He chuckled while admitting that he had perhaps overreacted a bit the day before. *Ya think?*

For the final activity, Max and I went on a cattle drive while the kids hung back at the lodge. Riding on horseback, we were tasked with moving a herd of about one hundred cows from one pasture to another. The organizers ask that you concentrate on the herding and not take any pictures, explaining that the guides would take the photos and AirDrop them to us at the end of the three-hour excursion. Not knowing what to expect, I'll admit it was thrilling. At the end of the ride, we were invigorated and energized.

As we got in the van to return to the ranch, one of the guides informed Max that she would AirDrop the photos to him. Sometime later, we headed to lunch to revel in our adventure and go through the pictures with the kids. Much to my surprise, there were no photos of me. Every one of the forty-five photos was of Mr. Greenfield. You heard me, not *one* photo of me. I swear I was there, living my best cowlady life. But then why would Mr. Greenfield need pictures of the nanny wrangling cattle? It was so absurd, we howled with laughter. "I am invisible!" I shouted, but still a tinge irritated.

All in all, the trip was a great bonding experience for the four of us. We laughed a lot, and everyone was pushed a little outside their comfort zone. This trip certainly reinforced who I was currently, viewed through others' eyes. The universe, way out there in all that gorgeous nature that made everyone feel small, mirrored my feelings of being perceived as nothing more than the wife of Mr. Greenfield, and in some cases, not even that.

In the past, I had been amused by people taking an interest in Max. I was secure, knowing our shared past, how hard we'd worked to get to that point, how much we adored each other and supported each other. I had always exuded an attitude of self-reliance, and I longed to occupy that place in the world again. Was it even possible to regain that same level of confidence without my fancy job title? Why did I feel ashamed to only be a wife, a mother, a daughter, a sister, a friend? On top of which, I felt ashamed that I was ashamed. Could those roles alone ever fill me up, or would I only be happy climbing the corporate ladder?

I do know that I will never be able to fully embrace just being Max's plus-one. The same drive that once brought me job satisfaction still lives in me and will help me to find my way. But just as I would never let my role as a wife solely define me, I had to learn that my career shouldn't either. And the more comfortable I became with my new reality, the easier it was becoming to reclaim that space. Max and I are a unit, comprised of two fully formed, equal individuals taking it on one day at a time, together.

13

Callbacks for Sexy Mamis: Recurring Guest Star

My girl Joyce (think Reese Witherspoon) is my neighborhood go-to. We talk husbands, kids, and dogs; diets, beauty, and sleep; work, heartbreak, and aspirations. She is equal parts safe place and hilarious sounding board. Over our ten-year friendship we have shared many highs and lows.

When I broke my left ankle while roller-skating with our kids, I drove from the rink to her house to pick her up before going to the emergency room. And she called me from the back of an SUV while going down a mountain in a life-threatening blizzard to bid me farewell, just in case. And when there was a guinea pig incident involving second-degree murder witnessed by both our kids, we trudged through that emotional aftermath together. (Joyce used the experience as inspiration for an episode of the TV show she created, *Single Parents*, so all was not lost.)

I am Joyce's YES friend—she says, "Tess?" I say, "Yes . . ." Doesn't matter what the ask is. How lucky that fate put us six houses apart, in what both our households refer to now as North and South Campus. We trade recipes and share place mats in a crunch, we each have a son and daughter, and spend Halloween at my house and Labor Day at hers; we share a handyman; our husbands text when the power is out, the Wi-Fi is down, or a package is dropped at an inopportune time; and we have four dogs between us—even they get along.

Joyce and I have a tradition of Friday night happy hour, which we call *Sundowners*. We have guest stars from time to time, but it always takes place in the kitchen at one of our houses. We drink skinny margaritas and graze over a cheese plate while recapping the best and worst moments of our busy week. We know all the same players, so no context or preamble is required; Joyce always gets it and can join any thought midstream. She will politely question my rationale, and I will gently nudge her toward boldness. We know our respective roles.

Recently Joyce expressed some anxiety about an upcoming "Mom and Son" spring break vacation to Hawaii with five other fourteen-year-old boys and their moms.

"What could be better," I thought. "He has his friends; you have a perfect group of lady moms."

Still, I sensed trepidation. As we walked our dogs around the block, I said, "It seems like you are not excited for your trip."

"I think 'dreading' is a good word for it," she admitted.

I had a feeling I knew what was going on. Her son had changed in the last year as he'd entered middle school. It was a phenomenon I'd seen before: sweet, adorable kid gets phone, downloads Snapchat, becomes unrecognizable a-hole.

"Billy hasn't made direct eye contact with me in two years,"

Joyce explained. "The only time he speaks to me is if he's asking for money, a ride, or to buy him a giant hoodie he found online. If I try to make conversation with him, he acts like he's in a youth detention center, scanning the exits for an escape."

"I feel you; Lilly has forbidden me from asking her friends any questions when they're in the car. I am an unpaid, silent Uber driver. Why don't you try a different approach with him? There's nothing sullen teenagers hate more than being interrogated. Why not try cultivating an air of indifference and let him come to you?"

"I've tried. I get one-word answers or nothing at all. It's 'yes, bro . . . no, bro . . . chill, bro . . .'"

"I have a pitch for you: Play the European Sexy Mami role on vacation."

I first discovered the Sexy Mami concept in my early twenties. I was on what would be one of the last vacations I would take with my parents. It might sound weird to be traveling with your parents as an adult, but I was newly single, and my parents were living in England, so I had not seen them in over a year. Also, I had just broken up with Topher and banged him for the last time to "Clocks" by Coldplay. To this day, any song from *A Rush of Blood to the Head* conjures memories of late-night romps with Topher and scurrying home in the early-morning hours.

On December 23 we arrived in sunny, warm Morocco. My dad insisted on carrying all three passports and presenting them at the immigration window upon landing. We were traveling as a unit, and he was the commander in charge of this vacation voyage. I enjoyed being able to coast on autopilot, not having to worry about any details, in exchange for the small price of being treated like a fifteen-year-old. This teenager was on board to explore the sights and sounds of North Africa.

We filled our days with a mix of excursions to open-air markets, local cafés, as well as tennis clinics and relaxing. The place where we stayed was decked out for Christmas and seemed to be welcoming families from all over Europe. This was not a season-one-of–*White Lotus* type of place. On a scale of one to fancy, this resort was a four; the staff, on the other hand, was a ten. It was comprised of exotic women and more male hotties than my eyes could take in, all dressed in white shorts and tight white polo shirts.

One of the first things I did after we settled in was book myself a massage at the hotel spa. *Sex and the City* was a hit at the time, and I was channeling my inner Samantha—it seemed like something she would do when vacationing in Morocco after a breakup. I was so happy to spend quality time with my mom, I insisted she come along and get a massage as well. We checked into the spa together; it was plastered white concrete with an arched doorway and smelled of eucalyptus. The sound of running water echoed all around.

"Hello, we are here for two massages; reservation is under Sanchez."

"Ah yes, madams," the receptionist said, as two young, handsome male massage therapists, dressed in that same uniform of white shorts and white polos, came from the back to lead us down a tiled hallway. It was almost comical how drop-dead gorgeous these two were, their sculpted bodies right out of *Magic*

Mike. I gulped as I locked eyes with the one with dark wavy hair slicked back, tanned skinned, and clear green eyes; we both held the stare a second too long. *I'm supposed to get naked in front of this dude?* A heated debate in French began as they showed us to the women's locker room to change. In hindsight, I'm guessing their exchange went something like:

"Hey, dude. I will take the younger one."

"No way, bruh, I just massaged that old Swiss guy. I need a break. Lemme take the younger one. I'll give you dibs on the next three appointments."

As my mom and I filed into the locker room to undress and slip into our robes, my mom said, "Oh, these robes are so soft. Do your slippers fit?"

I was already in a daze, still thinking about that *look*. "What? Slippers? They're fine, and yes, this robe is soft. Are we supposed to be naked?"

Just then a female spa attendant answered, "S'il vous plaît, madam, remove all clothing, undergarments, and jewelry and keep in the locker."

"Okay, merci," I said.

As we exited the locker room, the hunk who'd made the intense eye contact looked at me and smiled, as he gestured toward a private massage room. I guess my guy won the argument. *Oh my*, I thought, nervous with anticipation.

I heard the heavy wooden door close behind us, as we entered a steamy and dimly lit room, smelling of floral oils. He mimed instructions to disrobe and lie face down. In America, the masseur leaves the room and waits outside the door while you settle in, but not here. He just stood there next to the table, smiling. *Okay, I guess he is not leaving,* so I dropped my robe and lay down tushy-up on the table.

My face was now in the donut-shaped pillow, eyes wide open, staring at the floor. I heard him pull the massage oil from a harness around his waist, squeeze the plastic bottle and rub his hands together. He said in a whisper close to my ear, "Deep breath avec moi," and then put his hands just under the face rest so I could breathe in the aromatherapy. "Together, encore." Another deep breath followed by the long exhale. My inhibitions were melting away by the second. Then his very soft and strong hands began at the base of my back and glided up my spine to the nape of my neck. Instant electricity began pulsating throughout my body; he paused to pour more warm oil onto my bare back. Thank God my face was buried in the donut; I was giggling in total disbelief. *We* just *started, and this already feels so intimate and intense. How is this happening?* Something about being on this trip with my parents, and my mom being two doors down, made me feel like I was going to be busted and then get grounded. *Am I an adult? Oh, right, I am. I live on my own in an apartment where I pay rent.*

As he continued to massage my back, I could feel his breath deep and close on my bare skin. *He seems* really *into this,* I thought. Then, his hands made their way down my legs, to my calves (thank God I shaved), massaging along the way, before moving back up to my thighs, really working on the hamstrings, outer thighs, middle thigh, higher. *THIS IS CRAZY!* I thought, as he moved toward the inner, upper thigh, getting closer to my pot of gold than they would ever venture in America. *Umm, there's no way . . .* deep inner thighs . . . *wait, is this actually . . .* deeper inner thigh . . . *about to happen?*

"Dis okay?" he whispered in my ear in a thick French accent, with his hand right on the border of Oklahoma and Texas, then paused, awaiting my response, which came out in a breathless, "YES, dis OKAY!" With permission granted, his fingers plunged deeper. JACKPOT.

Any lingering thought of Topher and the breakup evaporated right there on the table in that Moroccan hotel spa. And every ounce of sexy confidence I ever had was restored in one climactic moment.

The massage went on, and my body was further explored. He remained in service, stationed in boner-city, with his white pants standing by at attention, begging for deployment. My time on this sub-Saharan expedition went over the allotted seventy minutes. At the end, he whispered, "Merci." *No, really . . . merci to* you. I put the robe back on, feeling a lot more like Samantha Jones in *Sex and the City,* and reunited with my mom back in the ladies' lounge, flushed and glowing.

"How was your massage?" my mom asked. "Yours was so much longer than mine."

"Relaxing, but deep—he really got in there."

Okay, thank you for taking that kinda dirty walk down memory lane with me. Now back to the Sexy Mami part. That evening, feeling rejuvenated and seated with my parents for dinner, a glamorous Spanish family swanned into the resort restaurant. Mom, Dad, three sons and one daughter, all teenagers ranging in age. Their festive gust of energy was intoxicating. Ever the acute observer, I noticed how they all circulated around the matriarch. She looked to be in her late forties, gorgeous, strong, and in command. She was Euro chic, in a sheer, floral, plunging neckline wrap dress, with kitty mules, slender, dark hair pulled tight in a chignon. It all looked effortless, but also impossibly perfect. The kind of look Americans can rarely, if ever, pull off. The husband pulled the chair out for his wife, and all the kids fought to be seated next to her. She was comfortable in her own skin, radiating warmth right back at them. There was no making space for her, she owned that space; she was the sun and her kids and husband clearly revolved around her.

I was so struck by the whole scene, all I could think was, *I want THAT someday.* It was a far cry from the forced American family vacation dinners I had witnessed, where the kids fight to sit furthest away from the adults, rolling their eyes because they can't wait for it to be over. I wondered how this inspired family dynamic I was witnessing had formed.

Just then, live calypso music began to play, and the mother stood up as two of the boys leaped for the first dance with her. I watched as they danced, but could not put my finger on her essence. What was it about her that made her so irresistible, so captivating? Then she threw her head back and laughed at something her son said, and I watched him spin her around.

Hold up . . . are those *sexy* vibes she's giving? It was almost like she was flirting with them. It wasn't sexual, but there was definitely something coquettish happening. Yes, she was attractive, but it was more than that. She possessed an inner beauty, a knowingness. The husband also gazed at her with affectionate eyes. I couldn't take my eyes off her either. They all wanted her attention, and she was doling it out like pieces of candy. It was a whole vibe.

Was this a cultural phenomenon? Does this matriarchal family dynamic exist only in southern European countries? What is this child-raising secret they possess? It made a lasting impression on me. During the rest of the trip, I began to really observe an elegance and freedom that these Euro mommies had. That family dynamic in the restaurant was not unique; I began to notice it everywhere.

When the trip was over, I left feeling so refreshed and inspired. I got to spend some much-needed quality time with my parents, which always grounded and recharged me. I had a secret spring in my step from my sexy French massage tryst, and a newfound impression about what kind of family dynamics were possible. With all that new insight and experience, I returned to LA, and about four weeks later, I met Max.

I was recently scrolling through Instagram and stumbled onto a video of a woman living in Spain who was sharing parenting tips for European child-rearing. Unlike kid-centric America, their philosophy is that life revolves around the parents, not around the children. If they have a late dinner at a café, the kids go with them. If they have friends over for a party, the parents don't rush everyone out the door when the kids go to sleep; the kids learn to sleep to the sound of their parents living their best lives. It starts at home. You want to go out to dinner with Mom and Dad? You order off the grown-up menu. There's no asking if your kids could just get plain noodles without sauce; you're too busy tearing it up on the dance floor.

I continue to struggle with this concept in my own life. I am guilty of making two separate dinners because my kids won't eat what the adults are eating. I am not unaware that I have cultivated a dynamic between mother and child that is one of unchallenged and continual "life waiter." *Yes, I will make that, drive you there, give you this, rearrange my life and goals so that you, child, remain number one on the call sheet of life.* How do we love and appreciate our children without losing ourselves? Enter Sexy Mami.

As I explained the idea of adopting this new persona to Joyce on her mother-son trip, she was hesitant at first. But staring down the barrel of five days in Maui with someone who rarely spoke in complete sentences to her, she decided to give it a try.

"Okay, Joyce, from the minute you board that plane, you are no longer Doting Mother; you are Sexy Mami. And you are going to have to abide by a new set of rules."

"*Oui, oui, mon amour,* I am in," she said with a perfect French accent, pretending to smoke an imaginary cigarette as I explained the rules to her.

1. Your answer on the trip is always "yes," regardless of what you would normally agree to and how dumb an idea it may be.
2. Be impressed and enchanted by everything he says.
3. Throw your head back and laugh at his jokes.

4. Stay out late—or not, just do you.
5. Encourage his independence.
6. Don't ask too many questions.
7. Own sexy indifference.

And last, but most important:

8. Speak to him like a peer.

Joyce was silent for a moment as she took it all in.

"What if he is rude while ordering? Can I correct him?" she asked.

"No, you are his friend, not his disciplinarian on this trip. If you want him to really see you as an ally and a whole person, then you need to act differently than you normally would toward him."

Like a perfect student, Joyce the Sexy Mami boarded that plane.

Extra dessert? Yes! Stay out late with the boys? Yes! When he called her "bruh" or grunted instead of using words, she laughed like she found it hilarious and charming. Gradually, the icy wall her son had put up began to thaw.

By day five, Joyce the Sexy Mami was feeling so confident, she even tried to engage her son on a dance floor like the original Euro-Mommy had done. Joyce, outfitted in a floral Isabel Marant short-tiered dress, motioned to Billy to join in. She turned her back to the dance floor and faced Billy, who was seated, grooving backward, miming as if she were pulling him to his feet by a rope while dancing to the beat. As Taylor Swift's "Shake It Off" blasted, she succumbed to Tay Tay's beat, proceeding to the center of the floor. Had I been there, I would have suggested for her to slow her roll; this seemed like running before you walk. An acceleration to the next level that he was not quite ready for. But to her credit, Joyce played through and was able to get a full dance party started, owning her own space, unafraid of what he might be thinking. Despite not getting him to his feet, Billy seemed genuinely impressed his mom could still raise the roof when she wanted to. She was having fun, full of vitality and joy, throwing caution to the wind. He was seeing her in a new light.

In the year since their trip, things between mother and son have been different. They have become buddies again, and that road to repair began with five days as Sexy Mami. I am not recommending a full-time Sexy Mami persona, but vacations are the perfect time to loosen the reins and let your hair down.

When I think back to the person I was before having children, I was interesting and relevant and daring—very much unlike how Lilly and Ozzie see me now. But that's what we sign up for, is it not? The thankless but ultimately rewarding role of motherhood? I agree that there is nothing more uninteresting than checking to make sure your child has done their homework or made their bed or cleared their dishes. I *do* think the mundane day-to-day aspects of parenting steal your personality, charm, and in my case, sense of humor.

Well, maybe not *all* my humor. I certainly laugh at my own absurdity and the lengths I go to sometimes to get it right. Whether you are a working mom or stay-at-home mom, it's the plight we all share. We fight, push, remind, and nag our kids to work hard and be thoughtful, kind citizens—even if that means putting our inner Sexy Mamis on hold for a bit. The nagging homework-checking mom in me, despite my aspirations toward sexy indifference, is alive and well. I am perched just beyond your bedroom door with my red pen, scanning for wet towels on the floor.

Joyce and Billy, on the other hand, have really figured it out. They are closer than ever. #MomGoals.

14

Exit Strategy:
Releasing the Breakdown

The majority of my childhood summers were spent in sub-urban North Dallas. The movie trailer version of a typical weekday would open on a raw egg being cracked on a hard surface by two small hands. Pull back to see the egg sunny-side up on the pavement, as my sister and I attempt to fry it on the 104-degree sidewalk in front of our house. The dry summer heat was like trying to breathe in an infrared sauna without all the antiaging skin benefits.

This would be followed by a slow-motion montage set to Gloria Estefan's "Rhythm Is Gonna Get You," of us walking to Taco Bueno or Crystal's Pizza to play video games with saved quarters, laughing as we rode bikes to our friends' houses to go swimming in their backyards, and rounding out with us roaming around the Galleria, an air-conditioned indoor mall. That about summed up summer, with its "entertain yourselves" vibe, as both of our parents worked.

When I was eight, my parents opened our home for a sec-ond time to a twenty-year-old German exchange student named

Heike, who was trying to learn English and was sorta supposed to keep an eye on us. Before Heike, there was Berget, who lived with us for two years, from when I was three years old to five years old. Berget loved me, and I have memories of lying in her arms in the backyard, enveloped by enormous breasts and ginger-red hair; she was the real-life Arielle, mermaid-like. Heike had straight, long brown hair and was also blessed with big tatas, but she had more of a Meadow Soprano look. She was taking classes at a nearby community college, but most of her learning came from the American boyfriend she quickly landed. She met him at the Mobile station while pumping gas.

My sister and I spent our evenings torturing these young lovebirds during their make-out sessions while parked in front of our house. We would open the horizontal venetian blinds and Christina would work the overhead lights like a strobe from her station at the light switch, while I wrapped my arms around myself with my back to the window and mimicked making out. Then I would either dance or work on my prat falls.

Oh, Heike, I am sorry for our unrelenting antics. All she wanted to do was sunbathe topless to "99 Luftballons," and we cramped her style. Heike lived with us for about eighteen months before returning to Germany. Her purple bikini bottoms that tied on each side left more of a lasting impression than her mastery of the English language. But she did introduce us to Milli Vanilli's "Girl You Know It's True," so we thank you UUUU.

By the summer between my eighth and ninth grades, we had relocated to California, and that was the end of my carefree summers. Instead I got my first job, scooping ice cream at Baskin-

Robbins. My new California bestie, Ryan, worked at Froglanders Crepes & Yogurt just down the street. Her work uniform was a pair of white Levi's with a tight, cute T-shirt with a tiny frog emblem over her (already C-cup) right boob. Comparatively, my uniform was a brown, pink, and orange horizontal-striped polyester dress that buttoned up the front, with a brown Baskin-Robbins baseball cap that fell just over my eyes. I looked like a misfit from the *Stranger Things* gang, behind the tall counter, shouting with a slight Texan accent through a mouthful of braces, "Hi, welcome to Baskin-Robbins"—picture Sydney Sweeney from *Euphoria*, then imagine the polar opposite . . . and that was me. Painfully out of place and underdeveloped.

Christina worked down the street at McSnack, a mini Mc-Donald's, wearing her very own brown polyester dress uniform and crowing in an even stronger southern accent, "Hi! Welcome to McSnack. Can I take your order?" Neither of the Sanchez sisters have taken a summer off work since, although the jobs did get better. The next summer Christina moved up to a gelato shop, and I moved on to Brooklyn Pizza.

But I really hit my stride when Ryan left Froglanders and we opened a flower stand out of a shack in a parking lot, which we named Scentsations. We were sixteen years old and were ready to get out of the food and beverage scene. Ryan had been eyeing the deserted shack, and we jumped on it. We thought, *why* not *us*? We knew where to buy the flowers in North County for wholesale prices. We were officially entrepreneurs . . . until a demolition crew made us aware of their plans to knock down the shack to do construction on the restaurant and parking lot. Soon we had a weekly flower delivery service with about twenty-five steady customers. They would put a vase out on their front step for us to fill with our signature bouquet every Friday, and we would collect the check left there for us made out to "Scentsations."

Though I look back fondly on all my summer adventures, from Dallas to California, I would have killed to go to sleepaway camp. The only camp Christina and I attended was cheer camp at the famous Southern Methodist University in Texas. It was one week of twelve-hour days learning cheer routines and gymnastics, in high ponytails and a year's worth of hairspray. Not exactly what traditional camps offered.

That is why I consider the idea of my kids going to summer camp an incredible privilege, and nonnegotiable. Mind you, this is not an entirely magnanimous position. I also do not want the responsibility of figuring out how to entertain and support my kids through various developmental milestones on my own. That's what school and camp are for. I outsource these things for a reason. And that reason is: I am neither good at taking on those responsibilities, nor do I want to—a perfect storm of inability meets disinterest. So, camp for Lilly and Ozzie it was!

As the camp drop-off approached, our beloved, sweet rescue dog, Joey, started showing symptoms of the fatal cancer he had been diagnosed with the previous August. We adopted Joey from a high-kill shelter during the pandemic, and he quickly became our family security blanket. Always interested in snuggling, he would race to lick the tears off your face, which in my case was often.

Joey was nine years old, missing teeth, had scars on his nose, and an ear filled with dense scar tissue. He was like an old character actor you love seeing, kind of like Walter Matthau (same nose). Ozzie and Joey were best friends. Joey sat next to Ozzie during homeschool and watched many a dance party in the kitchen. Anyone with a dog knows these little buddies crawl into your life and directly into your heart. Losing one is devastating at any age.

At the time of the diagnosis, he was given three to four months to live. It was now three months past the six-month mark, and Max and I were grappling with when the right time would be to put him down. The doctor told us he was too old and sick to endure chemotherapy or surgery to shrink or remove the tumors. As his cancer became more aggressive, we had to admit to each other it was finally time. I was absolutely convinced that losing this dog was going to scar Ozzie for life, and possibly kill Max.

After much lamenting, Max and I made the anguishing decision to put Joey down after we dropped the kids off at the bus for camp. We reasoned, too, that this would not come as a total surprise to Lilly and Ozzie. Both kids could sense Joey was in rapid decline. He could barely make it around the block on most walks, but bless his soul, he never stopped perking up and waging his tail at the sight of them.

Oh, and Max and I are cowards. Could I get an adult over here to help navigate this situation? Where're my grown-ups at? Max and I have, of course, navigated adult decisions before, where one of us has taken the lead to guide the other through uncharted waters. But this situation called for a real grown-up.

"It's not fair we have to make this decision," I said to Max while stomping my feet like a child. Joey had been so strong for our family and loved us through so much heartache and loss. "I can't deal with more sadness and pain."

Also, the timing sucked. Our kids were going away to camp and would be someone else's problem/gift for two whole weeks. This was supposed to be a sexy escape for Max and me. I was planning to channel Heike the foreign-exchange student, committed to topless sunbathing in the backyard and making out with Max to German rock music, but nothing kills a vibe like nursing the ailing pet you consider part human.

Camp day had arrived, and my adrenaline was through the roof. Was Ozzie going to be okay? Was I a bad mom for not telling the kids that Joey would not be here when they returned? Was I cheating them of the opportunity to say a proper goodbye? I flash forward to Ozzie in therapy as a twenty-two-year-old, blaming me for his inability to maintain intimate relationships because people and pets disappear. Out of pure guilt, I would be paying for that therapist and Ozzie's rent until he was forty-five, minimum. Lilly wouldn't bother with therapy; she'd find closure by marching directly into a new life, Anna Delvey–style, never to be heard from again.

Alas, there was no time to fixate on it; we had a camp bus to catch. The drop-off location was about forty-five minutes away. My stomach was in knots. *God, I cannot wait to pry that effing cell phone out of Lilly's hands*, I thought, as I watched her take a selfie with her tongue out and making a peace sign with her fingers. With no small amount of satisfaction that my thirteen-year-old was about to enter two phone-free weeks, I told her it was time for a *digital detox*.

Lilly laughed out loud. "Digital detox? What is that—a drink? A diet?"

I looked at Max in disbelief, as if to say, *What have we done wrong?* He kept his eyes on the road, refusing to engage.

"No, it means that you give up, in your case, the toxic-level use of your phone, tablet, computer, anything that is digital," I said, looking back at her, wanting to regale her with stories of my blissful screen-free summers, but knowing I would be met with a blank stare.

Lilly's like a small mob boss, except with that bewildering lack of common sense that only a self-assured thirteen-year-old can possess. She is unapologetically confident in her understanding or lack of understanding of life. It reminds me of the time she claimed there was no hot water but was only turning on the cold faucet. Was I out sick the day of parenting when you teach your children LEFT IS HOT with the capital *H* etched into the handle, RIGHT IS COLD with the capital C, like it has always been in homes across America? (She wouldn't last a week at Baskin-Robbins.)

Halfway up the 101, I felt a serious rumbling in my stomach. I asked Max, "Can you pull off and find a gas station? I need to use the restroom." Lilly protested and said, "We don't have time; we can't be late!"

This felt like an emergency, so Max exited the freeway and pulled into the first gas station. I jumped out of the car, feigning calmness. After handling my business, I washed up and headed back to the car; it was a tight three minutes. The kids were brimming with anticipation. "Sorry for the pit stop. Let's get to those buses." Back on the road, I sighed with relief.

We approached a football field–sized parking lot of a deserted mall in Woodland Hills. The streets were empty except for a steady stream of cars filing in with excited parents and campers. It was already eighty-five degrees at seven a.m., and the temperature was climbing. I was brimming with excitement for my upcoming kid-less freedom, nerves for Ozzie's first time away, and total dread for the afternoon of grown-up responsibility and the heartbreak of losing Joey.

We spilled out of the car and walked to the check-in line for name tags and bag check. There was a flurry of people milling around. I took Ozzie's hand and held it tight. *You got this!*

My stomach then made a noise I can only liken to that of a heavy wooden door being slowly opened in a cartoon haunted house.

"Owww, whoa," I said, wincing.

Max asked, "What's wrong? Did you forget something?"

"No, my stomach is, ohhhh, cramping," I said, hand on my gut.

"Do you need to go to the bathroom?" Max asked, as more audible fireworks came from my stomach.

"No, I'll be fine. All good," I said, grimacing.

Max shot me a look of concern.

At this point, trying not to double over from the pains that started shooting below my waist, I was beginning to doubt my confidence as the crowd of many familiar faces grew. One mom approached. "Are you excited?" I couldn't make eye contact with her. My mind said, *Tess, be present, your family needs you right now, smile, you can do this.* But could I? I felt my body temperature rising as sweat drops trickled from my temples. I realized in a split second that maybe, in fact, I *can't* do this.

"Max!" I yelped in an elevated tone. "I am going to find a bathroom."

"Yes, go. Go!"

Walking with purpose, eyes locked straight ahead, I started moving in a combo speed walk/run toward the deserted mall that looked straight off the set of *The Last of Us.* I finally made it to the entrance and grabbed the door handle despite seeing a chain and dead bolt firmly attached. I frantically rattled the door, hoping it would open. I pulled on the chain harder, letting out a whimper. Nope. Okay, running to another door, trying that door. Where the eff is Pedro Pascal to blow the door open and direct me to a sanitized bathroom with soft toilet tissue and elevator music? *Por qué, Pedro, por qué?*

I began talking to myself. "Oh God, oh God, oh God, why is this happening?"

This was a lower intestine coup d'état. Riots were happening on every street of my stomach; chaos reigned. A revolt at the highest level—buildings were crumbling inside my body. I looked around in sheer horror, no Pedro to save me, and nowhere to hide as I clenched every fiber of my body. I had to keep holding on as I glanced back at all the kids and parents. They didn't deserve to see a grown women in this epic battle, just throwing her possessed body against a row of several locked doors.

This fight was moving into phase two: recognition that I was going to lose this war. The panic started to dissipate as I moved toward acceptance. Could I really surrender to this unthinkable fate? The fate that bad dreams are made of? I looked around the parking lot, searching for any shred of coverage—a bush, a wall, a dumpster—nothing. Just parked cars, buses, parents, and campers. If I had a white flag in my pocket, I would have raised it and fallen to the ground in surrender.

I turned around and began my walk of shame through the crowd in my black leggings and short yoga tank in quiet despair as my bowels trumpeted: *See ya later, sis. We outta here.*

It felt like I heard a loudspeaker across the parking lot with a robotic female voice: "Evacuate. Vessel will combust in ten, nine, eight . . ."

While I couldn't see what was happening in my pants, I imagined it looked like a large black steam train angrily leaving a tunnel and smashing into a wall made of Dri-FIT stretch fabric. This is the most violent revolt my stomach has ever committed. *Ever.* It was a full system meltdown. The dam had broken and filled my pants as I walked expressionless toward Max's truck.

Was it even unlocked? I don't know. Was there extra clothing in there? Not sure. What are you going to do? Don't know. My sights were laser-focused on getting to his truck and trying desperately not to think about what was in my leggings. Along the way, a few people tried to speak to me, but I was a speechless zombie.

I finally got to the truck and reached for the handle of the back seat door as time stood still. Thank God it was unlocked.

I flung the door open, sat down directly on the rubber mat on the floor, and began to catch my breath as I dialed Max.

"Where are you?"

"I am in the back of your truck, on the floor."

"What? Why? Are you okay?"

"No, I am not okay, not at all. I shit my pants."

What came next was the sound of Max hysterically laughing. He laughed so hard for so long. Kevin Hart would kill for that kind of robust, sustained, legit laugh. It was a laugh so deep and honest, it probably added six months to his life. I have given vaginal birth to two children in front of Max and never questioned the future of our intimacy. Until that day. Would he ever stop laughing, and could our relationship as lovers survive this?

"How are the kids?" I asked.

Max handed the phone to Ozzie while he continued to laugh.

"Mom?"

"Hey, Bud, I'm sorry I darted off. I had to find a bathroom. You good? You're going to have the BEST TIME. I love you."

"I love you too, Mom."

I know that my son loves me, but he had no idea I was calling him from the floor of a truck, resting in my own hot mess. Will this knowledge change him? He probably won't read this until well into his twenties, when, as previously discussed, he'll have a therapist to help him process it all, so I at least have a solid decade or more of his affection and respect before he realizes his in-control, cool mommy, despite her best efforts, could not hold her potty. Max took the phone back. "They're getting on the bus now. I'll be back as soon as the bus leaves."

About twenty minutes went by. It could have been five or forty-five, I don't know. I was lying flat, face up, legs over the center hump, with my feet on the other floor mat. I had transported myself to another universe. I had already planned to start a new life in a small village on my own, far away. Yes, I would miss Max and the kids, but after this fiasco, how could I resume my life as a capable human?

I quietly hid on the floor of Max's truck. I say "hid" because he does not have tinted windows. Anyone who walked by could peer in. Just being caught huddled on the floor of my husband's truck during camp drop-off would be weird enough, let alone if people knew why I was there. *Don't mind me*, waving them off, on a phone call I would mime through the window, pointing to a phone with no one on the other end.

I was pulled back to reality when Max opened the door and got in. He looked back at me lying on the floor and tried to withhold his laughter. He said just one thing: "Tess, you choosing to sit on the rubber mat instead of the fabric seat is one of the most thoughtful things you have ever done for me."

Getting a salsa stain out of fabric seats will run you fifty bucks at an auto-detailing place. Can you imagine what they'd charge for this absolute catastrophe? But honestly, I can't take credit for being "thoughtful" during this crisis. I was in survival mode.

I didn't look up, I just muttered, "Please drive home now." We pulled out of that crime scene of a parking lot with all four windows rolled down and began the forty-five-minute drive back home. My head rested on the side of the seat, my eyes closed, horrified. And then I remembered the veterinarian who was going to euthanize Joey in just a few hours. Could this day get any worse?

We pulled into the driveway. I asked Max for the keys to the house and said, "I am going to get out of this car, walk to the front door, go inside and directly into the bathroom. You are not to move until you hear the front door close. Please do not look at me or talk to me. You don't know me. Please leave a black trash bag outside the door for my clothes, which I will be burning. And I will be showering until further notice."

Max tried to say "understood" without laughing, but I could hear in his voice how amused he was by all of this.

Exhausted, I proceeded to dispose of my poopy pants and shower with the ferocity of Meryl Streep in *Silkwood*, frantically scrubbing away all but the embarrassment. I needed to put on a clean pair of big-girl pants and prepare for the next worst thing that was about to happen.

The vet and an assistant arrived and spoke in hushed tones while Joey tried to get up and welcome them. We moved to the couch, where Max and I draped our bodies over Joey, with my ear pressed tightly to his back. I felt my head rising and falling with each of his breaths. Losing his big barrel body and unique-to-him canine smell filled me with unimaginable grief. Max and I sobbed, holding each other's hands as we nestled into him. After injecting him with the second shot of poison, the vet quietly said, "He is crossing over now."

My head no longer moving with his breath, Joey and I were still. So very still. He was free from his diseased body.

Max and I spent the next twelve hours in our quiet house,

void of kids and sweet Joey, holding each other, sort of frozen. After the traumatic parking lot incident, the digestive revolt, and the well of tears I cried for Joey, I was empty.

Following the initial shock of losing Joey dissipated, Max and I did get to spend some quality time together. Not topless sunbathing, Heike-level, but good enough. And on the plus side, post–angry bowels incident, I had never looked thinner or more glowing. I am talking the kind of svelte glow you can only achieve after five days at a detox spa.

Missing Joey, we decided to foster a rescue dog. Enter Darlene, a middle-aged, dark-haired beauty. If Darlene were a person, she'd be from Philly, work the front desk of a motel, and speak with a cigarette dangling from her mouth: "How long you staying, hon?" I couldn't help but feel that she was heaven-sent from Joey—she exudes the same rare, loving essence and gratitude. We would not make permanent decisions on adoption until the kids returned and met her, although we were very hopeful and falling for her quickly.

As Max and I returned to the parking lot, the scene of my intestinal meltdown, we rehearsed and rehearsed how we were going to tell the kids about Joey. Lilly got off the bus first and ran into our arms. "Oh my God, you look taller and more mature. Where is Ozzie?" He spotted us and ran over, and we laughed and hugged. Luggage and campers in tow, we piled into Max's *pristine* truck. It cost a ton, but a CSI forensic team would not be able to pull a speck of my DNA from that back seat.

Before we even left the parking lot, Ozzie said, "I can't wait to see Joey." Max and I were flopping around like teenagers, trying to talk about anything but Joey, even though we knew we had to get into it before we reached the house.

We pulled into the driveway, turned the engine off, and I took a deep breath. "Guys, remember how we said Joey was really not doing well before you left?"

Silence as they both looked at me wide-eyed.

"Well"—Max and I were both facing the back seat now—"Joey passed away in his sleep. Joey died. Joey is dead." *Okay, Tess, stop talking.*

Max said, "His body gave out and his cancer took over. He loved you both so much."

Lilly immediately started crying. Ozzie was glassy-eyed and quiet. I could see Einstein-like equations above his head, trying to make sense of this emotional algorithm, his face desperately trying to process these heavy words.

Through her tears, Lilly said, "Can we get another dog?"

Both Max and I said yes at the same time.

Through more tears: "When?"

"Well, we are fostering a dog right now," I said. "We hope you'll like her. Her name is Darlene, and she's inside."

Both kids immediately sat up straight. "Wait, what? A new dog's inside?" Lilly asked.

"Now?" Ozzie said.

"Yes, right now."

They both jumped out of the car and raced to the house. I unlocked the front door to find Darlene wagging her tail just inside, so happy to meet them as they showered her with love and affection.

I'd hoped they would fall in love with Darlene right away, but I wasn't quite sure how they'd take the news about Joey. And they seemed . . . fine. Does that make them psychopaths or emotionally resilient kids? I really don't know. I was anticipating wading through a lot more emotional wreckage, yet things seemed kind of okay.

Is this the reality of adulting? Making tough decisions on behalf of our children? We worried so much about Lilly's and Ozzie's emotional transition from Joey to Darlene, and it was fairly seamless. They both loved Darlene immediately and fully, without ever looking back. Although Max and I felt like inept teenagers—tortured by both the decision to put Joey down and how to tell the kids—we were learning that our job as parents was not to try to control their response, but just to be there for the aftermath, however it played out.

Sometimes it takes shitting yourself in broad daylight in a packed parking lot to learn to loosen the reins and relinquish control. And in hindsight, I am grateful Pedro Pascal didn't save me at the mall. Pedro and I are destined to have a future together, and let's be honest, starting our affair under those circumstances would have made things weird. Llámame, Pedro.

15

End Credits

In December 2022 we moved my mom and dad into their new home at Piper Sands, a senior community. My sister and I tackled the job together. After three days of intense labor—lifting furniture, rolling out rugs, and unpacking boxes—they were settled in to begin the next chapter in this "simplified living situation," as I'd dubbed it.

Before leaving Los Angeles, I ran to Target to stock up on holiday decorations for my parents. I purchased a little Christmas tree and decorated it with their favorite ornaments and colored lights. I added a wreath with twinkling lights to the front door, bought fresh flowers and pine branches for the table centerpiece, and ordered food to be delivered on Christmas Eve for breakfast the next morning—baskets of muffins, cookies, and bagels. I was determined to make their first Christmas in their new home filled with loads of holiday cheer, especially since we wouldn't be there that year to celebrate with them.

As I was leaving, my mom handed me a few file folders packed with photographs, documents, and newspaper clippings.

I tossed them onto the passenger seat of my car without a second thought and hit the road. I was literally and metaphorically racing toward the end of December to Christmas and a new year—2023 felt like an opportunity for us all to start a new chapter.

Upon returning home to Max and the kids, I was giddy with excitement as we prepped for our Christmas getaway. Months before, we had booked a return to one of our favorite places in Mexico. We were leaving an unseasonably rainy and cold winter in Los Angeles, and as soon as we landed in the eighty-degree heat, my shoulders slowly began to creep down from my ears and settle back into their rightful place. There is no question that I am warm-blooded. My DNA dictates that I am meant to live in the sun. It feels almost physically impossible for me to be happy in the cold.

We flew to Mexico on December 25, and as soon as we checked into our hotel, we changed into bathing suits and headed to the beach. I took a deep breath, and an enormous sense of relief washed through me. For the first time in two years, I was not beating myself up. I wasn't anxious, I wasn't thinking about job prospects or a lack of them, my parents were settled, and I was living in this glorious space, in the moment, with my little squad of four.

That Christmas Day was magnificent. Max and I lay together on the beach, watching Lilly and Ozzie frolic in the waves with unfettered joy. I thought nothing on earth could make them happier in that moment, and then, in the distance, we saw parachutes. It was Santa with his elves. Never has Saint Nick been greeted with more enthusiasm than on that beach, surrounded by a crowd of eager, cheering kids. Ozzie lined up to have his picture taken on Santa's lap. He is a big-time believer, or so he says.

We ate dinner and ended the perfect evening of a perfect day by calling my mom and dad, passing the phone around so that we could each wish them a Merry Christmas. My mom shared with me their plans for the rest of the week, and the many people they were going to see. As hard as their move had been, I was so happy we had stayed the course. I liked their new living situation because they seemed, dare I say it, happy. We turned in early that night, exhausted but with hearts full of gratitude.

The next morning, Max and I popped into the gym at the resort before breakfast. I had the Beyoncé album blasting in my AirPods as we smiled at each other from across the floor. Just then, my phone rang. I saw it was my mom, which was weird, given how it was only eight o'clock. I barely got out my greeting before she said, "Tess, Dad is dead."

"WHAT?" I screamed so loud that everyone in the gym paused as I dropped my phone, accidentally hanging up on my mom. No! How could this be? I had just talked to them fifteen hours ago. I was completely stunned. I raced out of the room and called her back, with Max chasing me, catching me, and wrapping me in his arms as I asked, "Mom, what happened?"

She explained that while she was out walking the dog, Dad had gotten out of bed and hit his head on the nightstand. She returned from her walk just as the paramedics arrived (the home health aide had already called them), but Dad had passed before they showed up. "Oh my God. Nooooo!" I somehow dredged up the words: "Are you okay?" She just began to weep and asked me to please call my sister, as she hadn't been able to reach her. I said I would, and we hung up. Max held me tight as I wept in his arms in the bright sun.

I rummaged around in my brain for some wisdom, looking for the solace I desperately needed in that moment. "He wanted this; he wasn't happy, he was done; he didn't want to be here, right? This is a blessing, right? This was not the life he was meant to lead. He was ready." Max just held me tighter. I tried to imagine my dad lying there with his spirit leaving his weak body and broken mind. "He's free now. He is finally free." My words tumbled out with my tears, almost trying to convince myself of their truth.

I tried calling my sister a couple of times. She, too, was in a different time zone in Hawaii, and it was a while before she called me back. "Hey, sorry, I was on a hike," Christina said. "I have five missed calls from you. What's up?"

"I'm so sorry to be calling and telling you this. Dad died this morning."

Christina gasped. "What? How?"

"He fell and hit his head."

She was quiet. We stayed on the phone, silent. I was still in shock. I knew she needed a minute to process the awful words I had just spoken. Trying to comfort us both, I finally said, "I know it feels too soon and unexpected, but maybe he wanted this. He needed to get Mom settled in their new home before he left." She listened, and we cried together. We both felt frozen in time in that moment.

My next call was to my sweet *tío*. Ron picked up the phone immediately. "Tess, yes, I know. I just spoke to your mom. I am so sorry. You know he loved you so much. He was so proud of you."

"He left us a long time ago. Just his body was here," I replied. "He is free now, right?"

Ron answered reassuringly, "Yes. He deserved more than he could squeeze out of life." Then he added, "He was my best friend," and we both started crying.

Exactly twenty days after their first night in their new home, my dad's withering body checked out. I think he chose the day after Christmas to leave this earth so as not to steal any focus from future Christmas days. Always so thoughtful and courteous, he never wanted to inconvenience anyone. I am relieved there was no hospital stay, no IVs, no artificial pumping of his heart, no intubation to help him breathe, no choices to make about whether or not he would want to prolong his life for even a minute. He left on his own terms. I believe he took control and that he had a pact with himself: *Enough is enough. My family is safe and settled. My work here is done.*

Ozzie came running into my arms upon hearing the news and sobbed. My boy and my dad had a quiet understanding between them, uncluttered by words. Ozzie knew he was a loving haven. He would just walk up to Pablo and hug him. They were bonded together in a way I don't believe either could have described. Maybe language would have complicated what they both knew and felt—that incredible genetic familial connection.

Lilly took time to process it, and hugged me for such a long time, squeezing so tightly. She spent the next couple of days checking in on me and reading my eyes as she does so well. At the beginning of every meal, Max insisted we each take turns saying something about Pablo, a memory, or something we were grateful for. Ozzie said he loved Pablo's hugs and the pantry full of snacks. Lilly loved that he had played the piano with her.

That night, as we finished up dinner, I saw a cluster of familiar faces enter the dining room. My longtime friends from my early scouting days, Casey Wilson and June Raphael, and their families had booked stays at the same resort. We had spoken in early December, so I knew that they would be there at the same time, but I think in all the chaos, I had forgotten. I ran to them with my arms open, welcoming the ever-present levity and warmth that follows them into every room. I told them about my dad's passing that morning. I will never forget June reaching out her hand and making a circular motion six inches over my heart—erupting with empathy, she said, "Protect this."

I was able to spend the next afternoon with Casey and June, floating in the lazy river, with piña coladas in hand. Ever so seamlessly, they coaxed my ruminating sadness into laughter. Something I thought at the time would be impossible. Over the next five days, as our families milled around the resort, they always made space for me, pulling up a chair, inviting me into their circle. We talked about true crime stories or as June calls it, the dark arts, TV and movies. We even shared a New Year's Eve dance on the beach surrounded by our children. They generously offered me a reprieve from my overwhelming grief, a gesture that I remain eternally grateful for.

We flew home, and I started to share the news with a few friends. My sweet gays showed up, reached out, stopped by. They brought candles, food, and wine. They called, sent emails, and made more calls. I felt less lonely taking shelter in their comfort. Almost all of them had met my dad through the years, and they shared their different memories with me. Some stories made me laugh and others brought me to tears.

One friend reminded me that when their son was two years old and my dad happened to be in town on Halloween, he had donned a black cape, hat, cane, and long gray wig to hand out candy, scaring the little ones so much that I had to ask him to take it off. I had forgotten until then, and was reminded that he had, in fact, become more playful and relaxed in his later years.

Other friends told me he always gave them such great advice: "I reached out to him for his opinion about this offer. . . ." "My brother called to ask for his take on that job opportunity. . . ." I was amazed as I learned of all the people he had helped, and of all my friends who had sought his counsel. Their memories flooded me with warmth, sadness, and beauty—such a mix of emotions. I felt as though I was held in some kind of odd suspension.

As I was unpacking my suitcase at home, there in the back of my closet were the file folders my mom had set aside for me in early December when I was helping them move. I grabbed them, and a few photos fell out. I sat down and paged through stacks of letters and emails I had sent my dad over the last twenty years, which he had printed out and saved in his office files.

My parents had moved to New York and then England during and after my college years, so this was how we had stayed connected through different time zones and busy work schedules. I sat for the next several hours reading the letters from my younger self to my dad, all addressed to his AOL account with a date and time stamp. I could not believe that he had saved them. I remember writing to him a lot, but I could hardly recognize my own voice. I ended many of the emails with "What do you think?" and was again reminded of how much I had sought his counsel and approval over the years.

I discovered several emails explaining to him how I'd met this cute guy named Max. It was like time traveling. I was right back there, communicating my life to my dad. It was wild to read some of these letters about Max and the early observations I had of him: "I know it doesn't make sense on paper, but he is so kind, and he melts away all my worries, especially when it comes to stressful work stuff. Max just smiles and says, 'God, I adore you.'"

Life at that point felt pure and filled with infinite possibility. Another one from fall 2003 read: "Max is an artist, effortless in his creativity. It's frustrating that I can't always harness it. He is, at times, just Maxie, simple and sweet, and other times he's so complex and layered. He is both things in one package. He is not like anyone I have ever met. I believe he is destined for something so much bigger in this life."

I paused after reading and turned to Max. "I have really loved and believed in you from the beginning." It was poetic.

Some of these emails included Dad's responses back on the same page. One said, "I just read this email and I love your descriptions. I hope you keep writing; maybe you should look into taking a writing class. Maybe a second career path awaits."

Reading that took my breath away. Maybe my dad knew one day I would need to read these emails to tap into the scrappier, twentysomething version of myself, to locate the younger me who was unafraid and ran toward challenges, not from them. What a gift to be transported to that time in my life with my dad as my witness. An archive of memories was waiting for me: my dad's voice, still so vibrant and full of wisdom on the page, my initial love for Max spelled out; it was all meant to be.

My dad knew I would be back for those memories when I needed them the most. Here he was, advising me even now. I needed to remember my relationship with my dad as it was and as he was. The kind, loving force of life, encouraging me to always keep reaching.

One painful favor had certainly turned into a few more, but even in all the loss, I have grown so much through the pain and humility. If I had kept my job, maybe I would have missed the opportunity to be with my dad in his final months. Maybe I would have missed this window to be there for Lilly and Ozzie, to show them what vulnerability looks like and that I am not invincible, but that I also know how to be strong.

I lost the woman I thought I had to become, the one driven by what I thought I had to be. Now, I realize I'm still connected to her, but I have also reconnected with the person who wrote those emails to her father, who was optimistic about life and the future.

I am on the other side looking beyond, feeling my dad all around me, urging me to greater heights as a more complete person than I was before. And when all is said and done, this is not how my story ends. A new chapter has begun.

State of Affairs:
STARS, Where Are They Now?

B y the time this book is published in 2025, Lilly Bird will be in high school, which feels impossible to believe. She even recently experienced having her first boyfriend (and will probably want to kill me for including that detail in these pages). The changes that take place between ten and fifteen years old are seismic. She is not a little girl but not yet a woman. (Thank you, Britney Spears, for articulating that so perfectly.) This age is supposed to be the most challenging time between a mother and daughter, but I think we have done really well, navigating it together. I begrudgingly need to give some credit to the fact that I have been around, A LOT. Just being present and available has helped, I suppose. Honestly, it is hard to get mad at her because, well, she too is a really good hang.

Ozzie will be in third grade then, so maybe time isn't moving that fast after all. Ozzie sounded surprised recently when I told him I used to have a job and go to an office every day. Umm, hello, have you not been here watching all this drama unfold? Nope. He does not remember a thing. To him I am and will always be life waiter, concierge, and chauffeur. That perception needs to change. Although I fight this at times, I do accept at this stage of his development, I am a means to an end. He is sweet, Dad obsessed, sporty, and still shy. I feel confident in saying that the best is yet to come for the two of us together.

Max is forever my cute boyfriend and my hands-down number one dinner companion. Aside from his sports analogies and obsession with basketball, we are on the same page about life's priorities and parenting. He makes me laugh, and insists that I laugh at myself on the reg. Our relationship is the single greatest thing that has happened in my life. I think he would say the same but would tie it with the free agency signing of Jalen Brunson to the New York Knicks. You get my point.

Christina reconnected on LinkedIn with a childhood family friend from Dallas with an invitation to lunch, which turned into dinner when both parties arrived to the table divorced and their taxi lights on. This hot affair has been going on for over a year, and she just announced she is moving out of Northern Cali to Texas to live with her new boo. I don't want to get ahead of myself, but I think this is IT. True love. And I could not be more thrilled about it.

There is also another hot couple alert, and this one we never saw coming.

My mom, still living in the senior community that she moved into with my dad before he passed away, was just beginning to acclimate to life as a party of one—a transition that Christina and I worried a lot about. Until one evening, she attended a classical music concert as part of a group outing and was seated next to a fit gent we will call "Clyde." Think an Alan Arkin type. Tall, handsome, and fit. They shared some pleasantries and learned that they lived just one floor away from each other in the same building. Clyde is a widower and had moved in in early January, so he was new to the campus. With some free time on her hands, she offered to show him around the following day—an offer he graciously accepted. That meet-cute turned into dinner with another couple they both knew. Ever so seamlessly, they found themselves at dinner together every night that week, concluding each evening with: "Same time tomorrow night?" Oh yeah. On my weekly calls with my mom, *I* conversations turned into *WE* conversations as their relationship continued to blossom.

On one of my visits, while I was in the lobby collecting some mail, a Piper Sands administrator approached. "Hi, are you Mrs. Sanchez's daughter?"

"Yes I am," I said.

"Your mother and Clyde have become a famous pair around here. They sure are keeping things lively. We asked your mom to please park her car in her assigned parking space over and over, but she kept insisting on parking in the guest parking lot. Eventually we moved her car ourselves. And then Mr. Clyde drove his car all over the multilevel parking garage while your mother hung out the window, clicking the remote as they searched for her car. Honestly, I don't think the car was still charged, but they were on a mission. Then they became convinced the car had been stolen and they called the police to file a report."

The vision of my mom hanging out the passenger window like Vanessa Hudgens in the movie *Spring Breakers*—a cherry lollipop hanging out of her mouth, pointing her key chain at every car they passed—while Clyde ripped around the garage floors, was one I could not easily get out of my head. Young lovers on the run. Outlaws. Like Bonnie and Clyde.

On our first Thanksgiving without my dad, Max and I hosted at our house and invited the new Insta-official couple. They arrived sharing one suitcase, so separate rooms were off the table. Gulp. The visit went well, complete with a Thanksgiving toast, made by Clyde.

"I would like to thank you for welcoming us into your beautiful home." (He said *US.*) "I am so grateful for this love right here—my sweetie, who I love so very much." They gazed at each other, my mom looking at him with loving eyes, and Clyde doting on his *girlfriend.* What is this, an episode of *Normal People?* They were giving off Connell and Marianne energy.

"Cheers!!" I said, then guzzled my entire glass of sauv blanc.

Let's unpack this for a moment, shall we? Are you as freaked out as I am? Does this seem too fast too soon? If you are thinking that, imagine how I feel. While news of this bombshell has settled a bit, I don't know how I am supposed to feel. My mom seems happy. And how lucky she and Clyde are to have found each other at this stage of life. Is it even my place to reject or embrace this romance? My role is to love and support my mom, right? And they do say that moving on and starting a relationship right after someone passes indicates that their last relationship was a healthy one. I know my dad would want nothing more than for her later years to be spent with someone who loves and adores her. Maybe Pablo even had a hand in bringing them together.

Does love and courtship feel different at eighty than it does at fifty and at fourteen? The star ladies in my life—my mom, my sister, and Lilly—are giddy and love drunk. I have to say I am enjoying the direction this is going.

As for me, after spending three and a half years beating myself up and feeling pretty shitty, I have carefully and slowly turned down the volume on that song. I miss my dad a lot, but often talk to him when I walk Darlene around the neighborhood. In terms of getting over losing my job and figuring out who I am without it, there were no shortcuts in my metamorphosis. Time eventually delivered me to acceptance. My job and the time spent building my career are and will always be a cherished part of me and my life. I am moving forward now in a new direction, preparing and ready for the next right opportunity.

Writing this book has generated a lot of gratitude for all my experiences and painful favors. Now I understand intimately you can count on change and the messy aftermath that results. The key to success, fulfillment, and happiness, in my opinion, is flexibility; embracing the now, however that may look. The obligation we have to ourselves is to water the flowers, not the weeds. Nurture and grow the good in your life, and dehydrate those motherfucking weeds.

With deep thanks, bye for now.

Call me. I want to hear about you and which new direction you are going.

Cue: Taylor Swift's "Sweet Nothing"

Spotify Playlist

https://open.spotify.com/playlist
/1ISCAV89QIczd7dTwmewdE?si=9294aac5896b4830

Acknowledgments

I want to thank my team at Gallery Books, especially my editor, Pamela Cannon, who from my first pitch expressed passion and vision for what this book could be. Your recurring note to find levity in the sorrow pushed me to dig for humor and irony when the tone was too heavy. Thank you for your guidance and for taking a chance on me. Thank you to Andy McNicol, who gracefully tempered my constant impatience and schooled me on the nuances of the literary and publishing world. To the brightest light and my candle in the dark, Jason Weinberg, who read the very first draft and immediately put this story into motion to become a book. Thank you for believing in me. And to Merritt, you know exactly why I am thanking you. LT, Queen of the East, thank you for the endless laughs and support, I am so glad Madonna brought us together.

Thank you to Tricia Boczkowski, my fast friend and grammar mentor; your intelligent insights challenged me and led me to be become a better writer. Thank you to the kind Margaret McKay, my Aussie pal, who listened to my words of grief and despair and always encouraged me to keep going.

Thank you to my mom and my sister, Christina, who gave

their blessing to share our family stories. Thank you to my tío Ron; you and Tom have made my life more colorful and brighter in every way. I don't know who I would be without your constant unconditional love and influence. Thank you, Jojo, for your unwavering belief in me and everything I set out to do. You are my favorite person and I am so lucky I get to call you family. Thank you, Marty, for always supporting me and for being the best grandpa to Lilly and Ozzie.

Thank you Ryan for your lifelong friendship; you are my sister, my origin, my heart. I am so grateful to have shared so many rich memories together and look forward to celebrating our future milestones to come. Together till the end, Ms. Michaels and Ms. Moretti. Thank you Brett and Collin, for adopting me and allowing me to be your camera lady. I am so grateful for all our wonderful times together. A special thank you to my dearest JJ, with your overflowing heart and astute humor you walked by my side and talked out my heartbreaks and humiliations until our shoes gave out. To Shannon, thank you for always holding out your hand to pull me up. Thank you Marcello, Jaime, Stephanie, and Becca, you all have played a role in my healing, I am so grateful for your support. To Jamie-Lynn, you set the bar for exemplifying grace in the face of challenge, thank you for showing us all how it's done. Thank you to Marc and Jackson. To my funniest friend, Kevin Christy, who will drop whatever he is doing in any time zone to workshop a single joke for well over an hour until we are both laughing too hard to speak. You get me, and I thank you. Thank you Charlie Andrews, our joyful times and laughter together are the medicine of life. Your support and friendship through my most stormy days have kept me grounded and feeling seen. I love you.

Thank you to the shiniest soul that flutters around me, Lilly Bird, and to my sweet Ozzie boy; I am so lucky to be your mom. You make me better.

To Maxie, thank you for insisting during a walk in Battery Park that I stop talking and start writing. It was unclear at the time if you were just fatigued from my incessant chatter or you actually thought I should write a book. Either way, I took your prompt and started to type.

I once heard from a tarot card reader that I had paid my love and relationship debts in past lives and this lifetime would be filled with the singular greatest love of all. Just so we are clear, I have earned this, I mean "us," and you are the bonus of my lifetime. I love you the most.

Author's Note

These essays are based on my personal experience of events. I have changed some names and descriptions and I have reconstructed dialogue to the best of my recollection. Some details may be recalled differently, but my sentiments about them are honest and true.

AUTHOR'S NOTE